Against the insidious wiles of foreign influence, the jealousy of a free people ought to be constantly awake, since history and experience prove that foreign influence is one of the most baneful foes of republican government.

George Washington,
Farewell Address

There are few things in the U. S. that Japanese want to buy, but there are a lot of things in Japan that Americans want to buy. This is at the root of the trade imbalance.

Akio Morita, Chairman
Sony Corporation

BUY

AMERICAN

WHO OWNS WHAT IN THE UNITED STATES

Annette Donoho
December 1991

Printed in the USA

TABLE OF CONTENTS

INTRODUCTION

Epilogue

Sources

Acknowledgements

INTRODUCTION

It's easier to say "Buy American" than to do it. Names and titles can be deceiving: Frusen Gladje is American, while the Loyal American Life Insurance Company of Mobile, Alabama, isn't. Reading labels is not the answer: Gold Medal Flour and Pillsbury Flour both list Minneapolis, Minnesota, as their home, but only one is American-owned. "Made in America" doesn't mean American either. Hondas, Sony TVs and Sanyo microwaves are made in the United States but are not American-owned. On the other hand, products of some American-owned companies, such as Plymouth Lasers, Dodge Colts, Zenith small TVs, and Kodak cameras, are not necessarily made in the United States.

So what is "American?" Officially defining what constitutes a "domestic" product or company is consuming huge amounts of legal time. The Bureau of Economic Analysis defines "American" as "any business enterprise that is not owned 50% or more by a non-U.S. citizen." However, that definition doesn't really work, because 50% is not required for a hostile takeover. In some cases where insiders only own a small percent, the question becomes, "where does the power reside?" For instance, the insiders of Clorox own only 1.6% of their company stock, and the largest stockholder with 28% is a German chemical company with a seat on the board of directors. The Securities and Exchange Commission and the International Trade Administration of the Commerce Department both set 10% ownership as "a controlling interest."

The basic premise that I have used in writing this directory is: where do the NET profits stay? If none of the net profits are sent over one ocean or the other, it's an American company.

This directory was not written to convert anyone. It is a guide for those who already feel, as I do, that we must support and preserve what is left of our American companies. Already there are more than 100 products - including VCRs, camcorders and bicycle tires that have NO American-owned companies. The television manufacturing industry has only one survivor, Zenith, and the tire industry has only Goodyear and a private label tire maker, Cooper.

We must buy American - while there is American left to buy.

Chapter 1

FOOD AND DRINK

FOOD COMPANIES

BAKING SUPPLIES

AMERICAN OWNED	FOREIGN OWNED	
Argo Corn Starch	.	
Aunt Jemima Pancake	.	
Betty Crocker Cakemix	.	
Bisquick	.	
C&H Sugar	.	
Duncan Hines	. Fleischmann's Yeast	Australia
Gold Medal Flour	. Hungry Jack Pancake Mix	England
McCormick Cake	.	
Decorations	.	
	. Pillsbury Cakemix	England
	. Pillsbury Chilled Cookie Dough	England
	. Pillsbury Flour	England
Red Star Yeast	. Revere Sugar	Phillipines

BAKING CHOCOLATE

Bakers	.	
Hershey's	. Nestle	Swiss
	. Toll House Chocolate Chips	Swiss

CANDY

Almond Joy	. After Eight	Swiss
American Licorice	. Alpine White Candybar	Swiss
Bar None	. Baby Ruth	Swiss
Big Hunk	. Bit-O-Honey	Swiss
Bounty	. Brach Candy	Swiss

	Butterfingers	Swiss
	Cadbury	England
	Calbee	Japan
Cella's Confections	Chuckles	Finland
	Chunky	Swiss
Charmes		
Chip Away		
Fifth Avenue	Fanny Farmer	France
Ghiradelli Chocolate	Goobers	Swiss
Godiva Chocolatier	Gummi Bears	Germany
Golden Almond		
Good News		
Hershey's	Heath	Finland
Junior Mints		
Kit Kat		
Krackel		
Kudo's		
Life Savers		
Look		
M&M's		
Mars		
Mason Dots		
Milky Way		
Mounds		
Mr. Goodbar		
New Trail	Nestle's	Swiss
Peter Paul	Oh Henry!	Swiss
	100 Grand	Swiss
	Payday	Finland
	Pearson	Swiss
	Power House	England
Reese's Peanut Butter	Ragold	Germany
Cups/Pieces	Raisinets	Swiss
Rocky Road	Rowntree	Swiss
Rollo		
Sees Candy	Sunmark	England
Skittles		
Skor		
Snickers		
Sugar Babies		
Symphony		
3 Musketeers		

Toblerone   .
Tootsie Roll   .   Turtles   Swiss
Twix   .
Vernell's Candy   .   Violet Crumble   Australia
Whatchamacallit   .   Whoppers   Finland
Whitman's Chocolate   .
Wrigley Gum   .
York Peppermint   .
   Patties   .

CANNED VEGETABLES AND FRUITS

AMERICAN OWNED	FOREIGN OWNED	
Apple Time	. A & P	Germany
	. Cantadina	Swiss
Del Monte	.	
Dole	.	
Empress	.	
	. Green Giant	England
Heinz	.	
Hunts	. Indian Summer	England
	. Libby's	Swiss
Musselman's	. Mott's Applesauce	England
Progresso Italian	.	
Imported	.	
S & W	.	
Stokley-VanCamp	.	
	. Western Foods	England

CANNED GOODS: BEANS

AMERICAN OWNED	FOREIGN OWNED
A & P	.
B & M Brick Oven	.
Campbell's	.
Franco American	.
Heinz	.
Hunt's Big John	.

		Libby's	Swiss
Nalley's	.		
Ranch Style Beans	.		
S & W	.		
Stokley's Van Camp	.		
VanCamp Pork 'n Beans	.		

CEREAL COMPANIES

AMERICAN OWNED		FOREIGN OWNED	
American Home	.		
General Mills	.		
Kelloggs	.		
Nabisco	.		
Post	.	Pillsbury	England
Quaker	.		
Ralston Purina	.		
Whitman	.		

COFFEE, TEA, AND COCOA

Brim	.		
Celestial Seasonings	.	Carnation	Swiss
Chock Full O'Nuts	.	Chase & Sanborn	Swiss
Empress Coffee	.		
Folgers	.		
General Foods Intl.	.		
High Point	.	Hills Brothers	Swiss
	.	Hot 'N Rich Chocolate	Swiss
	.	Lipton Tea	Unilever*
Maxim	.	Master Choice Coffee	Swiss
Maxwell House	.	MJB Coffee	Swiss
	.	Nestle	Swiss
	.	Nescafe	Swiss
	.	Nestea	Swiss
	.	Ovaltine	Swiss
Postum	.	Quick	Swiss

* Unilever is a joint venture of England and Netherlands

Sanka Brand	.	
Swiss Miss	. Sunrise Coffee	Swiss
	. Taster's Choice	Swiss
Yuban	.	
Coffee Rich	. Coffee-mate	Swiss
Cream White	.	
Cremora	.	
Pream	.	

CONDIMENTS, SALAD DRESSINGS, AND SPICES

AMERICAN OWNED	FOREIGN OWNED	
A-1 Steak Sauce	.	
Accent	. Adolph's	Unilever*
Bernstein's	. Baltimore Spice	Germany
Best Foods	.	
Bon Appetit	. Camino Real	Japan
	. Cattleman's Barbeque	England
	. Coleman's Mustard	England
Del Monte	. Diamon Crystal Salt	England
	. Durkee Red Hots	Unilever*
	. Durkee Sauces	Unilever*
	. French's	England
Good Seasons	. (spices/mustard/extracts)	
Grey Poupon	. Green Mountain Herbs	Canada
Gulden's Mustard	.	
Heinz	.	
(catsup/mustard/vinegar)		
Hellmann's	.	
Hidden Valley Ranch	.	
(28% Germany)	.	
Hunt's	. Indian Summer Vinegar	Japan
	. Italian Kitchen Vinegar	Spain
Kitchen Bouquet	.	
Knorr	.	
Kraft	.	
Lady's Choice	. Lawrey's	Unilever*
	. Lipton Salad Dressing	England

		Lea & Perrins	France
McCormack	.		
Miracle Whip	.		
Molly McButter	.		
Mrs. Dash	.		
Newman's Own	.		
Salad Dressing	.	Old Bay Seasonings	Germany
ReaLemon	.		
Regina Vinegar	.		
Rosarita Mexican	.		
Schilling	.		
S & W Vinegar	.		
Tabasco	.		
Weight Watchers	.	WishBone Salad Dressing	Unilever*
Worcestershire Sauce	.		

COOKIES

AMERICAN OWNED		FOREIGN OWNED	
American Collection	.	Animal Crackers	England
Barnum's	.		
Animal Crackers	.		
Chips Ahoy	.		
Dolly Madison	.		
Duncan Hines	.		
Entenmann's	.	E. L. Fudge	England
Famous Amos	.	Greg's	Taiwan
	.	Girl Scout Cookies (Wyndham)	Taiwan
	.		
Honey Maid Honey	.	Honey Grahams	England
Grahams	.		
	.	Jack's	Taiwan
	.	Jackson's	Taiwan
	.	Keebler	England
Mrs. Fields	.	Mother's Cakes & Cookies	France
Nabisco	.	Nestle	Swiss
Oreo	.		
Pepperidge Farm	.	Plantation (Wyndham)	Taiwan
	.	Shaffer Clarke & Co.	England

	. Town House Cookies	England
	. United Biscuit	England
Sunshine Vanilla Wafer.	Vanilla Wafer	England

CRACKERS AND BAKED GOODS

AMERICAN OWNED	FOREIGN OWNED	
Cheez-It	.	
Ding Dongs	.	
Dolly Madison	.	
Hi Ho	.	
Ho Ho's	.	
Hostess	.	
Honey Graham	.	
Krispy Saltine	. Keebler	England
	. Mother's Cakes & Cookies	France
Nabisco	.	
Pepperidge Farms	.	
Ritz	. Ry-Krisp	England
Sara Lee	.	
Sno Balls	.	
Sunshine Biscuits	.	
Sunshine Honey	.	
Grahams	.	
Twinkies	. Town House	England

DAIRY

The American government, both federal and state, has policies
that work against American businesses and favor foreign ones.
In 1985, the federal goverment pressured Georgia dairy farmers
to cut their milk production by 22%, taking 23,000 cows out of
production. The Georgia dairymen did not favor cutting the state's
milk production because there was no significant surplus of milk in
Georgia, but they did so nevertheless.

At the same time, the state government was wooing Masstock
International, an Irish dairy company, with promises of $4.5 million
worth of tax-exempt bonds, to move to Georgia and set up a dairy.

ICE CREAM & FROZEN BARS

AMERICAN OWNED		FOREIGN OWNED	
Avalanche	.		
Baker Ice Cream	.	Baskin Robbins	England
Ben & Jerry's	.	BonBon IceCream Nuggets	Swiss
Homemade	.		
Breyer's	.	Conello	Unilever*
Chipwich	.		
(45% Sweden)	.		
Dove Bar	.		
Dreyers Grand	.	Drumsticks	Swiss
Edy's Grand	.	Eskimo Pie	Swiss
Friendly Ice Cream	.	Foremost Ice Cream	Japan
Frusen Gladje	.	Gold Bond Ice Cream	Unilever*
	.	Good Humor	Unilever*
Herrell's Ice Cream	.	Haagen-Dazs	England
Jell-O Pudding Pops	.		
Kool Pops	.		
Life Savers Flavor Pops			
Lucerne Ice Cream	.		
Meadow Gold	.	Marigold Foods	Netherlands
	.	Nestle Bars	Swiss
	.	Nestle Crunch Milkbar	Swiss
	.	Popsicle/Fudge'sicle	Unilever*
Quality Check Ice	.		
Cream	.		
Sealtest Ice Cream	.		
Snickers Ice Cream Bar	.		
Steve's Homemade	.		
Ice Cream	.		
Tofutti Brands Inc.	.		
Weight Watchers	.		

* Unilever is a joint venture of England and Netherlands

YOGURT

AMERICAN OWNED	FOREIGN OWNED	
	. Alta Dena	France
	. Dannon	France
Golden Creme .		
Light 'N Lively .		
Sealtest .		
Tofutti Brands .		
Yoplait .		
TCBY .		

BUTTER, MARGERINE, AND MILK

Blue Bonnet .		
Challenge .	Country Crock	Unilever*
Darigold .		
Fleischmann's .	Foremost Dairies	Japan
Golden Creme Butter .	I Can't Believe It's Not Butter	Unilever*
.	Imperial Margerine	Unilever*
Land O'Lakes .		
Mazola .		
Meadow Gold .		
Nucoa .		
Parkay .	Promise Margerine	Unilever*
.	Queen's Farms Dairy (NY)	Canada
Saffola .	Shedd's Spread	Unilever*
.	Tuscan Dairy (Union, NJ)	Canada
.	Willow Run	Unilever*

CHEESE

.	Alta Dena	France
Borden .	Boursin	Unilever*
Cache Valley .		
Casino .		

* Unilever is a joint venture of England and Netherlands

Churney	.	
Cracker Barrel	. Dansk	Denmark
Fisher Cheese	. Frigo Cheese	England
Hoffman	. International Cheese Co.	Netherlands
	. (Vermont)	
Kraft	.	
Lake to Lake	.	
Philadelphia Cream	. Precious Cheese	England
Cheese	.	
Sargento	. Shedd's Foods	Unilever*
Sonoma Cheese	. Sorrento Cheese (Buffalo, NY)	France
Springfield	.	
Tillamook	.	
Velveeta	. Universal Foods of Milwaukee	Belgium

OTHER DAIRY PRODUCTS

AMERICAN OWNED   FOREIGN OWNED

Avoset   .
Cool Whip   .
Cremora   .
Dream Whip   .
Egg Beaters   .
Qwip   .
Reddi-Wip   .

DESSERTS

Banquet	.	
Betty Crocker	.	
D-Zerta	. Hostess Snacks	England
Jell-O	. Jus-rol Pastry	England
	. Knox Gelatin	Unilever*
Morton	. Mother's Cakes & Cookies	France
Mrs. Smith's Pies	.	
Pepperidge Farm	.	
Rich's	.	
Royal Pudding & Gelatin	.	
Sara Lee	.	
Tofutti Brands	.	

FROZEN FOODS

DINNERS AND MEAT

AMERICAN OWNED		FOREIGN OWNED	
Banquet	.		
Budget Gourmet	.		
Celeste	.	Chef Saluto	England
Chef Pierre	.		
Chicken By George	.		
ChunKing	.		
Groton's Seafood	.	Freezer Queen	Ireland
Gourmet Entrees	.		
Healthy Choice	.		
Hungry Man	.	Hungry Jack	England
Le Menu	.	Lean Cuisine	Swiss
Lightstyle	.		
Mary Kitchen	.		
Mrs. Friday's	.		
Mrs. Paul's	.		
Morton	.		
Old El Paseo	.		
Mexican Food	.		
Open Pit	.		
Patio	.		
Pierre Frozen Foods	.		
Professional Choice	.		
Snowking FrozenFoods	.		
Springfield	.		
Swanson	.	Stouffers	Swiss
Van deKamp Mexican	.	Van deKamp Fish Dinners	England
Dinners	.		
Weight Watchers	.		

FROZEN FOODS

VEGETABLES

AMERICAN OWNED	FOREIGN OWNED	
Birds Eye		
C & W		
	Green Giant	England
Kraft		
Ore-Ida		
Southland		
Springfield		
Stokely VanCamp		
Stokely USA		

PIZZA

AMERICAN OWNED	FOREIGN OWNED	
Celeste		
La Pizzaria	Jeno's	England
Pierto's Pizza	Totino's	England

JUICE

AMERICAN OWNED	FOREIGN OWNED	
Appletime		
Bodine's		
Chiquita	Carr	Swiss
Citrus Hill		
Country Time Lemonade		
Del Monte		
Dole	Everfresh	Canada
Gatorade		
Hawaiian Punch		
Hi-C		
Hunt's		
Kool Aid	Kern's Joice	Swiss
Kraft		

Martinelli	. Mott's	England
Minute Maid	.	
Musselman's	.	
Ocean Spray	.	
ReaLemon	.	
Seneca	. Sparkler	Canada
Springfield	. Sundance	England
Sunny Delight	. Sunkist	England
Sundor Brands	.	
Sunsweet	.	
Tang	. Tropicana	Canada
Treesweet	.	
Tree Top	.	
V-8	.	
Very Fine	.	
Welch's	.	

MEALS: CANNED AND PACKAGED

<u>AMERICAN OWNED</u>   <u>FOREIGN OWNED</u>

Armour .
Chef Boyardee .
ChunKing .
Dennison's .
Dinty Moore .
Franco American .
Gebhardt .
Hormel .
Hunt's .
La Choy .
Lunch Bucket .
Manwich .
Mary's Kitchen
Morton Hash .
Nalley's .
Old El Paseo Mexican .
    Food .
Spam .
Top Shelf .
Valley Fresh USA .

MEAT AND FISH

AMERICAN OWNED	FOREIGN OWNED	
Armour Foods	. Arbor Acres Farms	England
Banquet Chicken	. Ball Park Franks	England
Boyles	. Bumble Bee Tune	Thailand
Butterball Turkey	.	
Chick'n Quick	. Chicken of the Sea	Indonesia
Conagra Chicken	. Coral Tuna	Thailand
Cudahy Hams	. Fischer Packing	England
Eckrich	.	
Farmer John	.	
Foster Farms	.	
Glougherty	.	
Gold Kist Chicken	.	
Gwaltney	.	
Gallo Salame	.	
Hamilton	. Hygrade Food Products	England
Hillshire Farms	.	
Holly Farms Poultry	.	
Geo. A. Hormel	.	
Hubbard Chicken	.	
Hudson Foods	.	
Jennie-O Turkey	.	
Jimmy Dean Sausages	.	
Kahn's Weiners	.	
Little Sizzlers	.	
Louis Kemp Seafood	.	
Louis Rich	.	
Maple Leaf Farms	. Mid Pacific Tuna	Thailand
Morrell Meats	.	
Morton	.	
Mr. Turkey	.	
Norbest	.	
Ol' McFarlands	.	
Oscar Mayer	.	
Owens Country Sausage		
Patrick Cudahy	.	
Perdue Farms	. Peter Pan Seafood	Japan

Pilgrim's Pride Chicken .
Plantation Foods   . Quality Sausage   Unilever*
Rath Black Hawk   .
S & W Seafood   .
Smithfield Hams   .
Spam   .
Starkist Tuna   .
Swift   .
Tyson Foods   . VanCamp Tuna   Indonesia
Wilsons Foods   . Van deKamp's Frozen Seafood England

OILS

AMERICAN OWNED	FOREIGN OWNED
Crisco	
Hain Products	
Hollywood Brands	
Mazola	
Pam	
Planters	
Puritan	
Wesson	

PEANUT BUTTER AND JELLY
SUGARS, HONEY, AND MOLASSES

AMERICAN OWNED	FOREIGN OWNED	
Adams Peanut Butter		
Aunt Jemima Syrup		
Bama Jams		
Golden Griddle Syrup	Grandma's Molasses	England
Goober Jelly		
Jif		
JM Smucker Jams and Jellies		
Karo Syrup		

Knott's Berry Farm	.	
Kraft	.	
Log Cabin	.	
Lumber Jack	.	
Laura Scudders	.	
Mary Ellen	. Mrs. Butterworth's	Unilever*
Nutra Sweet	.	
Peter Pan	. Pacific Molasses	England
Simply Fruit	.	
Skippy	.	
Smuckers Syrups	.	
Springfield Peanut	.	
Butter	.	
Welch's	.	

PICKLES

AMERICAN OWNED	FOREIGN OWNED

Claussen Pickles	.
Del Monte	.
Heinz	.
Nalley's	.
Steinfields	.
Vlassic Pickles	.

SAUCES

Catelli Pasta Sauce	. Chris'n Pitt's Barbecue	England
Classico Pasta Sauce	. Contadina	Swiss
	. Camino Real	Japan
El Molino Foods	. Durkee Sauces	Unilever*
Golden Grain	.	
Healthy Choice	.	
Hunt's	.	
K.C. Masterpiece	.	
Barbecue	.	

* Unilever is a joint venture of England and Netherlands

Knoor	Lawry's	Unilever*
Las Palmas		
La Victoria		
Newman's Own		
Spaghetti		
Old El Paseo		
Old Smokehouse		
Barbecue		
Open Pit		
Ortega		
Pace		
Prego		
Progresso	Ragu	Unilever*
S & W Sauces	Spatini Spaghetti Sauce	Unilever*
Trader Vic's Barbecue		
Woody's Barbecue		

SNACKS

AMERICAN OWNED	FOREIGN OWNED	
Annie's Cheese	American Natural Snacks	Netherlands
Popcorn		
Borden's Cottage Fries	Butter Pretzel Knots	England
Chee-tos		
Cheez-It		
Cracker Jacks		
Doritos		
Eagle Snacks		
Fisher Nuts	Fiddle Faddle	Swiss
Franklin Crunch 'n		
Munch		
Frito-Lay		
Granny Goose Foods		
Hi Ho		
H & J Snackfoods		
Superpretzel		
Krunches	Keebler	England
Laura Scudder's		

Lay's Potato Chips	.	
Nalley's	. New Tech Snacks	England
New York Delichips	. O'Boisies	England
	. Pizzarias	England
Pepperidge Farms	. Poppycock	Swiss
Planters	.	
Pringle's	.	
Ritz	. Ry-Krisp	England
Ruffles	.	
Sunshine Biscuits	. Screaming Yellow Zonkers	Swiss
Tostitos	. Suncheros	England
Triscuits	. Tato Skins	England
Wheat Thins	.	
Wise Snack Foods	.	

POPCORN

AMERICAN OWNED	FOREIGN OWNED	
Act II		
	.	
Annie's Inc	.	
Betty Crocker Pop	.	
Secret	.	
Cracker Jack Popcorn	.	
Jiffy Pop	.	
Jolly Time	.	
Newman's Own	.	
Orville Redenbacher's	.	
Planter Premium Select.	Pillsbury The Original	England
Smart Foods	. Pop Deluxe	England
Weight Watchers	.	

SODAS

AMERICAN OWNED	FOREIGN OWNED
A & W Root Beer	.
Bubble Up	.
Coke	.

Country Time Lemonade.	Canada Dry	England
Crystal Lite .	Carr	Swiss
Cragmont .	Crush	England
Dad's .	Caselton Beaverages	Puerto Rico
Dr. Pepper .		
Gatorade .		
Hires .		
Koolaid .		
Mountain Dew .	Mott's	England
Mug Root Beer .		
Original New York .		
Seltzer .	Orange Crush	England
Pepsi .		
RC Royal Crown Cola .		
7Up .	Schweppes	England
Shasta .	Soho Natural Soda	Canada
Slice .	SunDance	England
Squirt .	Sun Drop Citrus	England
Sprite .	Sunkist	England
Teem .		
Upper 10 .	Wyler Powdered Drink	Netherlands
Vernors .	Yoo-Hoo Chocolate Drink	France

SOUP

AMERICAN OWNED	FOREIGN OWNED	
Armour Bouillon .		
Campbell's Soup .		
Heinz .		
Knorr .	Lipton	Unilever*
Pepperidge Farm Soups.	Maggi Bouillon	Swiss
Progresso .		
Swanson's Broth .		
Wylers Bouillon .		

* Unilever is a joint venture of England and Netherlands

STARCHES

PASTA

AMERICAN OWNED	FOREIGN OWNED	
American Beauty	. American Italian Pasta (MO)	Italy
Catelli Pasta	. Buitoni	Swiss
Chef Boyardee Pasta	. Contadina Fresh Pasta	Swiss
Creamette	.	
Del Monico	.	
Golden Grain	.	
Kraft	.	
Merlino's	.	
Misson Macaroni	.	
Mueller's Pasta	.	
Prince Pasta	. Pasta d'Vinci	Italy
Ronzoni	.	
San Giorgio	.	
Skinner	.	

RICE

Calrose	.	
Golden Grain	.	
Hinode	.	
Kraft	. Lipton	Unilever*
Minute Rice	. MJB Quick Rice	Swiss
Rice-A-Roni	.	
Uncle Ben's	.	

BOTTLED WATERS

AMERICAN OWNED	FOREIGN OWNED	
Alhambra	. Arrowhead	France
a Sante	. Belmont Springs	Japan
	. Caledon Springs	Swiss
	. Calistoga	France

	.	Clearly Canadian	Canada
	.	Crystal Springs	Japan
	.	Evian	France
	.	Deer Park	Swiss
	.	Kentwood	Japan
	.	La Croix Water	Australia
	.	Naya Natural Spring	Canada
	.	Ozarka	France
	.	Perrier	France
	.	Poland Spring	France
Rocky Mountain Water	.	Polar Water Co (Pittsburgh,PA)	Japan
Sparkletts Drinking	.	Sierra Spring Water (CA)	France
Water	.		
	.	Sunshine Water Co (FL)	France
	.	Victoria Springs (NJ)	Australia
	.	Zephyrhills	France

MAJOR PRODUCERS

AMERICAN OWNED		FOREIGN OWNED	
Campbell	.	Carnation	Swiss
Clorox (28% German)	.		
Duncan Hines	.		
General Mills	.	Grand Met	England
Hershey	.		
Kelloggs	.		
MM/Mars	.		
Nabisco	.	Nestle	Swiss
Phillip Morris/General	.	Pillsbury	England
Foods/Kraft	.		
Post	.		
Proctor and Gamble	.		
Quaker	.		
Ralston Purina	.		
S & W	.	Schweppes	England
Sara Lee	.	Unilever	England/Netherlands
Whitman	.		

* Unilever is a joint venture of England and Netherlands

WATER SUPPLY SYSTEMS

Arkansas
    Pine Bluff   France

Connecticut
    New Milford   France

Delaware
    Claymont (Suburban) France

Florida
    Jacksonville(Suburban) France

Idaho
    Boise   France

Illinois
    Lincoln   France

Indiana
    Lafayette   France

Maine
    Caribou   France
    Greenville   France
    Skowhegan   France

Missouri
    Jefferson City   France

New Jersey
    Lambertville   France
    Toms River   France

New York
    Great Neck   France
    New Rochelle   France

Pennsylvania
    Bloomsburg   France
    Bryn Mawr   France
    Harrisburg   France
    McKeesport   France
    Mechanicsburg   France
    Wrightsville   France

Rhode Island
    Wakefield   France

Washington
    Spokane (Suburban) France

AMERICAN WINERIES

AMERICAN OWNED	FOREIGN OWNED	
Acacia Winery	. Abbott Vineyards (CA)	Japan
(Napa Valley)	.	
	. Almaden Vineyards	England
	. (Madera, CA)	
Bartles & Jaymes	. Beaulieu Vineyards	England
(Modesto)	. (Napa Valley)	
Batavia Wine Cellars	. Beringer Vineyard	Swiss
(New York)	. (Napa Valley)	
Boone's Farm	. Buena Vista Winery	Germany
(Modesto)	. (Sonoma)	
California Cooler	. Charles LeFranc Cellars	England
(San Joaquin)	. (Madera, CA)	
Carlo Rossi	.	
(Modesto)	.	
	. Chateau St. Jean	Japan
	. (Kenwood, CA)	
Charles Krug	. Chateau Souverain	Swiss
(Napa Valley)	. (Sonoma)	
Chateau St. Louis	. Clos du Bois Winery	England
(Missouri)	. (Sonoma)	
Chateau Ste. Michelle	. Christian Brothers	England
(Washington)	. (Napa Valley)	

Colony	.	
(Sonoma)	.	
Creekside Cellars	.	
(Sonoma)	.	
Corbett Canyon	.	
(San Luis Obispo)	.	
Delicato Vineyards	. Domaine Carneros	France
(San Joaquin)	. (Sonoma)	
Fetzer Vineyards	.	
(Mendocino)	.	
E J Gallo	.	
(Modesto)	.	
Geyser Peak Winery	.	
(Sonoma)	.	
Gibson Wine Company	.	
(Fresno)	.	
Giumarra Vineyard	.	
(Kern County)	.	
Glen Ellen Winery	.	
(Sonoma)	.	
Golden State Winery	.	
(Tulare County)	.	
Italian Swiss Colony	. Inglenook	England
(Sonoma)	. (Napa Valley)	
JFJ Bronco Winery	.	
(Stanislaus County)	.	
Jacques Bonet	.	
(Sonoma)	.	
F. Korbel & Brothers	.	
(Sonoma)	.	
LeJon	. Le Domaine	England
(Sonoma)	. (Madera County)	
J. Lohr Winery	. Los Hermanos	Swiss
(Santa Clara)	. (Napa Valley)	
Martini & Prati Wines	. Maison Deutz	Swiss
(Sonoma)	. (San Luis Obispo)	
Paul Masson	. Markham Winery	Japan
(Monterey County)	. (Napa Valley)	
Mirassou	. Monterey Vineyards	Canada
(Santa Clara)	. (California)	
Mogen David	. Mt. Veeder Winery	Germany
(New York)	.	

Robt. Mondavi Winery	Napa Ridge	Swiss
(Napa Valley)	(Napa Valley)	
North Coast Cellars		
(Sonoma)		
Parducci Wine Cellars	Peller Wines of California	Canada
(Mendocino)		
Petri	Petaluma Ltd.	Australia
(Sonoma)	(Oregon)	
Round Hill Cellars	Ridge Vineyards	Japan
(Napa Valley)	(California)	
San Antonio Winery	St. Clement Vineyard	Japan
(Maddalena)		
Sbarbaro	Simi Winery	France
(Sonoma)	(Sonoma)	
Sebastiani Vineyards	Souverain Cellars	Swiss
(Sonoma)	(California)	
Summit	Sterling Vineyards	Canada
(Sonoma)	(Napa Valley)	
Sun Country Cooler	Sylvan Springs	England
(New York)	(Madera County)	
Sutter Home Winery		
(Napa Valley)		
Taylor California Cellars		
(New York)		
Tyrolia		
(Modesto)		
Weibel Vineyards		
(Alameda)		
Wente Brothers		
(Alameda)		
Widmers Wine Cellars		
(New York)		

BEER

AMERICAN OWNED	FOREIGN OWNED	
	. Amstel Light	Netherlands
	. Asahi	Japan
Bader Brau	. Beck's	Germany
Ballantine	. Black Label	Australia
Brew 102	. Bohemia	Mexico
Budweiser	. Burgermeister	Australia
Busch	.	
Classic Dark	. Carling Black Label	Australia
Coor's	. Carta Blanca	Mexico
	. Colt 45	Australia
	. Corona	Mexico
	. Dos Equis	Mexico
Extra Gold	. Foster's	Australia
Falstaff	. Foster Lager	Australia
Genesee Brewing	. Guinness Stout	France
Boebel	.	
Haffenreffer	. Heidelberg	Germany
Hamm's	. Heileman Export	Australia
Herman Josephs	. Heineken	Holland
	. Henry Weinhard	Australia
	. Iron City	Australia
Jacobs Best	.	
Keystone	. Kingsbury	Australia
King Cobra	. Kirin	Japan
L.A.	. LaBatt's Blue	Canada
Lowenbrau	. Lone Star	Australia
Meister Brau	. Micheys	Australia
Michelob	. Molson Golden	Canada
Mickey's Malt	. Moosehead	England
Miller	.	
Milwaukee's Best	.	
Natural Light	.	
Old Milwaukee	. Old Fitzgerald	France
Olympia	. Old Style	Australia
Pabst Blue Ribbon	.	
Pearl	.	
Piels	. Rainier	Australia

Schaefer	. Rolling Rock	Canada
Schlitz	. San Miguel	Philipines
Stroh's	. Sapporo	Japan
	. Schmidt	Australia
	. Special Export	Australia
	. Stag	Australia
	. St. Pauli Girl	Germany
	. Steinlager	New Zealand
	. Tacate	Mexico
	. Tuborg	Australia

ALCOHOLIC BEVERAGES

BLENDED

AMERICAN OWNED	FOREIGN OWNED	
Hill & Hill	. Calvert Extra	Canada
Old Grand-Dad	. Kessler	Canada
Old Taylor	. Old Fitzgerald	England
Old Thompson	. 7 Crown	Canada
Sunny Brook	.	
Sunny Hill	.	

BOURBON

AMERICAN OWNED	FOREIGN OWNED	
Ancient Age	.	
(22% Japan)	.	
Barclays	.	
Barton	.	
BJ Holiday	. Calvert Extra	Canada
Early Times	.	
Gentleman Jack	.	
Imperial	.	
Jack Daniel's	.	
Jim Beam	.	
McCormick	.	
Old Crow	.	

Old Forester	. Potter's	Canada
StillBrook	.	
Sunny Brook	.	
Sunny Hill	. Walker's Deluxe	England
Ten High	. Wild Turkey	France

CANADIAN

AMERICAN OWNED	FOREIGN OWNED	
Canadian Ltd	. Black Velvet	England
Canadian Host	. Canadian Club	England
Canadian Supreme	. Canadian Mist	Canada
Corby's	. Crown Royal	Canada
Lord Calvert	.	
Northern Light	.	
Windsor Supreme	. Seagram VO	Canada

SCOTCH

AMERICAN OWNED BOTTLERS and/or IMPORTERS	FOREIGN OWNED DISTILLERS	
	. Ballentine's	England
	. Black and White	England
	. Chivas Regal	Canada
Claymore	. Cutty Sark	England
	. Dewar's	England
	. Glenlivet	Canada
	. J&B	England
	. Johnny Walker	France
Lauder's	. Long John	England
McCormick	. Old Smuggler	England
Newport	. Passport	Canada
	. Potter's	Canada
	. Scoresby	England
	. Usher's	Scotland
	. White Horse	Canada

GIN

AMERICAN OWNED	FOREIGN OWNED	
Barclays	. Beefeater Gin	England
Barton's	. Bombay	England
	. Boodles	Canada
	. Booth's	England
	. Calvert Gin	Canada
	. Fleishman's	England
Gilbey's	.	
	. Glenmore	England
	. Gordon's Gin	England
	. Hiram Walker Gin	England
McCormick	. Potter's	Canada
Sunny Hill	. Schenley	England
	. Seagram's	Canada
	. Tanqueray	France

VODKA

AMERICAN OWNED	FOREIGN OWNED	
Barclay's	. Absolut	Sweden
Barton's	.	
Crown Russe	. Denaka	Denmark
	. FinLandia	England
	. Fleishman's Royal	England
	. Gilbey's	England
	. Glenmore	England
	. Gordon's	England
	. Hiram Walker Vodka	England
Kamchatka	. Icy Vodka	Iceland
Karkov	.	
McCormick	. Popov	England
	. Potter's	Canada
Sokolov	. Schenley	England
	. Skol	England
Sunny Hill	. Smirnoff	England
Vladivar	.	
Wolfschmidt	.	

TOBACCO

AMERICAN OWNED	FOREIGN OWNED	
Alpine	.	
Benson & Hedges	. Barclay	England
Bristol	. Belair	England
Camel	. Capri	England
Cambridge	.	
Carlton	.	
Cartier Vendome	.	
Century	.	
Chesterfield	.	
Doral	. Dorado	England
English Ovals	.	
Eve	.	
Kent	. Kool	England
L&M	.	
Lark	.	
Lucky Strike	.	
Magna	.	
Malibu	.	
Marlboro	.	
Max	.	
Merit	.	
Montclair	.	
Newport	.	
Now	.	
Pall Mall	.	
Parliment Lights	.	
Phillip Morris	.	
Players	.	
Premier	.	
Pyramid	. Raleigh	England
	. Redman	England
	. Richland	England
Saratoga	.	
Salem	.	
Tarrington	.	
True	.	

Vantage   .
Virginia Slim   . Viceroy   England
Winston   .

PET FOODS

<u>AMERICAN OWNED</u>   <u>FOREIGN OWNED</u>

Ally Cat	. Alamo	England
Amore	. Alpo	England
Bonz	. Blue Mountain	England
Butcher's Blend	. Bright Eyes	Swiss
	. Buffet	Swiss
Cat Chow	. Chef's	Swiss
Chow	. Come 'n Get It	Swiss
Chuck Wagon	.	
Cycle	.	
Dog Chow	.	
Field 'n Farm	. Fancy Feast	Swiss
Fit 'n Trim	. Figaro	Thailand
	. Fish Away	Swiss
	. Fresh Catch	Swiss
	. Friskies	Swiss
Gaines	. Grand Gourmet	Swiss
Gravy Train	.	
Happy Cat	.	
Hartz	. Hearty Chunks	Swiss
Hill's	.	
Hi-Pro	.	
Kal Kan	. Jim Dandy	England
Ken-L Rations	.	
Kibbles 'N Bits	.	
Kit 'N Kaboodles	.	
Main Stay	. Mighty Dog	Swiss
Meow Mix	.	
Milk-Bone	.	
Moist 'N Meaty	.	
9-Lives	.	
One	.	

Pedigree .
Puppy Chow .
Puss 'N Boots .
Purina Gravy .
Recipe Brand .
Select Dinners .
Sheba .
Special Dinners .
Tender Vittles .
Thrive .
Vets Skippy .
Whiskas .

SUPERMARKETS IN THE UNITED STATES

AMERICAN OWNED		FOREIGN OWNED	
Acme Supermarkets	.	Alterman Foods	Belgian
Albertson's (510)	.	Applebaum's	Canada
Alpha Beta	.	Arnold's Inc.	Germany
American Fare	.	A & P	Germany
B & B Cash Grocery	.	Best Yet	Germany
(24 Stores Florida)	.		
Big Bear	.	Big Apple	Belgium
Bruno's	.	Biggs Food Chain	France
	.	(Cincinnati)	
Buttrey Food Stores	.	Bi-Lo Supermarkets	Netherlands
	.	Big Star	France
	.	Bormans	Germany
Consumer Warehouse	.	Carr Brothers	Canada
Del Champs	.	Dominion Stores	Germany
(110 stores)	.		
(Gulf Coast)	.		
	.	Family Mart	Germany
	.	Farmer Jack	Germany
	.	First National Supermarkets	Netherlands
Food 4 Less	.	Food Bazaars	Germany
Food Max	.	Food Emporium	Germany
Food World	.	Food Lion (668 stores)	Belgium
Fry's Foods	.	Food World	Germany

	Food Town Stores	Belgium
Gelson's	Giant Food Stores	Netherlands
(Los Angeles)		
Giant Food Inc.		
(148 stores/		
Washington DC)		
Grand Union		
(303 stores)		
Gristede's (NY City)		
Harris Teeter		
(130 stores)		
Jewel Food Stores	Kings Supermarkets (NJ)	England
Kroger (1235 stores)	Kohl's Food Stores	Germany
Liquor Barn	Lil Champ Food Stores	France
Lucky	Lowe Supermarkets	Belgium
Market Place		
Marsh		
Martin's (New Engl)		
Mayfair (Los Angeles)	National Tea	Canada
	National Supermarkets	Canada
P & C Food Markets		
(88 stores)		
Pantry Pride		
(39 stores/Florida)		
The Pantry (California)		
Piggly Wiggly		
Pathmark (142 stores)		
Price Chopper		
(62 stores)		
Publix Supermarkets		
Pavillions (Calif.)		
Purity Supreme		
(66 stores)		
Red Apple		
(58 stores/NY)	Ralph's (140 stores)	Canada
	Red Food Stores	France
Safeway	Sav-a-Center	Germany
	Shaw Supermarkets (Maine)	England
Shop 'n Save	ShopWell	Germany
(New England)		

Shop-Rite	South Ogden Super Duper	Germany
(194 stores)	(Buffalo, NY)	
Smith's Food & Drug	Super Fresh Food Markets	Germany
(98 stores)		
Spartan Stores		
Star Markets		
Stop 'n Shop		
Sun Foods (New Engl)		
Super Valu Stores	Thruway Super Duper Inc.	Germany
	(Buffalo, NY)	
Wons	Victory Markets (Norwich, NY)	England
Weis Markets	Waldbaum Inc.	Germany
Winn-Dixie		
(1227 stores)		

RESTAURANTS

AMERICAN OWNED	FOREIGN OWNED	
A & W	Acapulco	Japan
Arby's (2100)	Arby's (50 in California)	Japan
Bakers Square (145)	Baskin Robbins	England
Bennington's	Bombay Palace	Canada
Bob's Big Boy (235)	Brasserie	Japan
Bob Evans Farms (255)	Brumby's (Salt Lake City, UT)	Australia
Bojangles (156)	Burger King	England
Captain D's Seafood	Burger King (36 in Hawaii)	Japan
(588)		
Carl's Junior (484)	Charlie Brown's	Japan
Chart House (92)	Chili's (248)	England
Chichi's	Club Mars (New York)	Japan
Church's Fried Chicken	Country Towers (Florida)	England
Country Kitchen		
Dairy Queen (5100)		
Dennys		
Domino's Pizza	Dunkin Donuts (1850)	England
El Pollo Loco Chicken	El Paso Cantina (10/Calif.)	Japan
Farrells		
Golden Skillet	Ground Round	England
Hot Shoppes	Hard Rock Cafe (NYC/TX)	England

Howard Johnson	. Hosts	Hong Kong
Intl. House of Pancakes	. Hungry Hunter	Japan
JB's (119)	.	
Jack in the Box	.	
Jerrico (1500)	.	
Karmel Korn Shoppes	.	
Kentucky Fried Chicken	.	
Int'l. Kings Table (84)	.	
Lee's Famous Recipe	.	
Chicken (282)	.	
Long John Silvers	.	
(1500)	.	
Luby's Cafeteria (127)	.	
Lyon's Restaurants	.	
Marie Callenders	. Mama Leone's	Japan
Max & Erma's (18)	. Manchu Woks	Canada
McDonald's (10,720)	. Metro Restaurants	Japan
Morrison's Family	. Mister Donut (475)	England
Dining (169)	. Mother's Restaurants (Ohio)	Japan
Mrs. Fields Cookies	. Mountain Jack's	Japan
Nathan's Famous (69)	.	
Olive Gardens	. The Office	Japan
Orange Julius	.	
Pancho's Mexican	.	
Buffet (66)	.	
Perkins Family	.	
Restaurants (371)	.	
Piccadilly (126)	. Peachtree Restaurants	Hong Kong
Pizza Hut	. Pizzaland	England
Ponderosa (736)	. Prufrock Restaurants (Texas)	England
Popeye's Chicken	.	
Quincy's Steak House	.	
Rally's DriveThru (194).	Red Robin Hamburgers (57)	Japan
Rax Restaurants (440)	. Red Coach	England
	. Regi's Grill (14)	England
Red Lobster Inn	. Romano's Macaroni Grill	England
Reuben's (39)	.	
(So. California)	.	
Round Table Pizza	. Rothchild Restaurant (Hawaii)	Japan
Rustler (77)	. Roy Rogers (600)	Canada
Ryans Steak House	.	
(132)	.	

Sambo's (175)	.	
Shoney's (636)	. Seafood Broiler (California)	France
Sizzler (628)	.	
Spaghetti Warehouse	. Spencecliff Restaurants (HI)	Japan
Steak & Ale	. Stouffer Restaurants	Swiss
Steak N Shake (102)	.	
Straw Hat Pizza	. Stuart Anderson's Cattle Co.	England
Subway	.	
T. J. Cinnamon	.	
Bakeries (230)	.	
Taco Bell	. Taco Villa (Texas)	England
TCBY (2000)	.	
TGI Friday's (140)	. TGI Friday's (Portland/SEA)	England
	. Totino's	England
Village Inn Pancake	. Trader Joe's (30)	Germany
House (256)	.	
Wendy's (3754)	. Wimpy's (529)	England
Western Sizzlin (550)	. Winchells Donuts	Canada

CHAPTER 2

TRANSPORTATION

Foreign money does not generate jobs. Less than 5% of jobs that resulted from foreign money were NEW jobs, while the other 95% were EXISTING jobs in U.S. companies that were acquired by foreign investors. The TOTAL number of jobs did not increase, but more jobs came under the control of foreign bosses. Actually, the total number of jobs decreased - 36,000 were lost in 1988-89 alone. A United Auto Workers study states that for every job created by a foreign auto plant, three jobs are eliminated. These include jobs in assembly and in the auto parts industry, because foreign-owned companies import more of their parts - approximately $40,000 worth of goods for each worker employed, compared to American-owned businesses that import less than $3,000 for each worker. In 1964, UAW members built 98% of the vehicles made in the United States. By 1991, that figure was 59%.

FORD

MODEL   FACTORY LOCATION

FORD

Model	Factory Location
Aerostar Wagon (designed by Nissan)	St. Louis, MO
Bronco	Michigan
Club Wagon	Lorain, OH
Econoline	Lorain, OH
Escort	Wayne, MI / Hermosillo, Mexico
Explorer	Louisville, KY
Festiva (designed by Mazda)	Korea
LTD Crown Victoria	Wixom, MI
Mustang	Dearborn, MI
Probe	Flat Rock, MI (with Mazda)

Taurus   Chicago, IL / Ontario, Canada
   (engine by Yamaha Motor Co)
Tempo   Kansas City, MO/ Ontario, Canada
Thunderbird   Lorain, OH

LINCOLN/MERCURY

Continental   Wixom, MI
Cougar   Lorain, OH
Crown Victoria   Ontario, Canada
Grand Marquis   Ontario, Canada
Mark VII   Wixom, MI
Mercury Capri   Australia
Sable   Chicago, IL / Atlanta, GA
Topaz   Kansas City, MO / Ontario, Canada
Town Car   Wixom, MI
Tracer   Hermosillo, Mexico
   (designed in Japan)

JAGUAR   England

FORD TRUCKS

Bronco/Bronco II   Michigan, / Minneapolis, MN
Explorer   Louisville, KY
F Series   Norfolk, VA/ Ontario, Canada
Ranger   Louisville, KY/ Minneapolis, MN /
                          Edison,NJ/ Ontario, Canada
Super Cab   Minneapolis, MN
Light Ford Trucks   Kansas City, MO/ Norfolk, VA/
                          Michigan/ Ontario, Canada
Medium & Heavy Trucks Kentucky

GENERAL MOTORS

The GM plant in Fremont, California, closed in 1982 due to staggering absenteeism and crippling labor conflicts. In 1984, Toyota reopened the plant and rehired half of the original 5,000 workers. Absenteeism dropped from 20% to 2%, and grievances from several thousand to almost none. The plant operated at full capacity using half the workers. WHY??

BUICK

Century	Oklahoma City/Terrytown, NY/ Mexico
Electra/Park Avenue	Wentzville, MO
Estate Wagon	Lakewood, GA
LeSabre	Flint, MI
Reatta	Lansing, MI
Regal	Ontario, Canada
Riviera	Hamtramck, MI
Roadmaster	Arlington, TX
Skylark	Lansing, MI

CADILLAC

Allante	Body built in Italy/final assembly in Hamtramck, MI
Brougham	Arlington, TX
DeVille	Lake Orion, MI
Eldorado	Hamtramck, MI
Fleetwood	Lake Orion, MI
Seville	Hamtramck, MI

CHEVROLET

Astro	Baltimore, MD
Beretta	Linden, NJ/Wilmington, DE
Camaro	Van Nuys, CA
Caprice	Arlington, TX/Lakewood, GA/Willow Run, MI
Cavalier	Lordstown, OH/Janesville, WI
Celebrity	St. Terese, Quebec, Canada
Corsica	Linden, NJ/Wilmington, DE/Willow Run, MI

Corvette	Bowling Green, KY
Van	Scarborough, Ontario, Canada/Lordstown, O
Lumina coupe/van	Oshawa, Ontario, Canada/Terrytown, NY

OLDSMOBILE

Custom Cruiser	Arlington, TX
Cutlass Calais	Lansing, MI
Cutlass Ciera	Oklahoma City/ Quebec, Canada
Cutlass Supreme	Doraville, GA
88 Royale	Wentzville, MO/Flint, MI
98 Regency	Lake Orion, MI
Silhouette Van	Terrytown, NY
Toronado/Trofeo	Hamtramck, MI
Touring Sedan	Lake Orion, MI

PONTIAC

6000	Oklahoma City
Bonneville	Wentzville, MO
Firebird	Van Nuys, CA
Grand Am	Lansing, MI
Grand Prix	Fairfax, KS
Le Mans	Designed in Germany
	Re-engineered in Michigan
	Manufactured in Seoul, Korea
Sunbird	Lordstown, OH
TransSport	Terrytown, NY

SATURN

Every Saturn car is made entirely in Springhill, Tennessee, USA. 95% of the parts are American made.

GEO

Metro	Built by Suzuki in Japan
Prizm	Built by Toyota (with GM)
	in Fremont, CA
Storm	Built by Isuzu in Japan

Tracker	Built by Suzuki in Ontario, Canada
GM owns:	50% of SAAB
	100% of Lotus
	38% of Isuzu
	50% of Daewoo Motors, South Korea
	5% of Suzuki

GENERAL MOTORS TRUCKS

CHEVROLET TRUCKS

Blazer	Shreveport, LA/ Pontiac, MI
C/K Pickup	Pontiac MI/Fort Wayne, IN/ Ontario, Canada
Kodiak	Janesville, WI
Lumina APV	Terrytown, NY
RV Blazer	Flint, MI
S10	Lordstown, OH/Shreveport, LA
Suburban	Flint, MI

GMC

Jimmy	Moraine, OH/Shreveport, LA/
S15	St. Terese, Quebec, Canada,/ Oshawa, Ontario, Canada/ Shreveport, LA
Safari Van	Baltimore, MD
Sierra Pickup	Ontario, Canada
Sonoma	Moraine, OH/Shreveport, LA
VanDura	Scarborough, Canada/Lordstown, OH

CHRYSLER

Foreign competitors set up "screwdriver factories" in the United States to circumvent American anti-dumping laws and European import quotas. "Screwdriver factories" assemble foreign-supplied parts into final products, leaving research, design and the manufacture of expensive components, in the foreign country. The low-skill and therefore low-wage jobs are performed in the United States.

By slapping on a "Made in USA" label, these manufacturers are able to slip through import limits and quotas set by other countries.

CHRYSLER

Grand Caravan	St. Louis, MO
Grand Voyager	St. Louis, MO
Imperial	Bellevedere, IL
LeBaron	St. Louis, MO/Bellevedere, IL
New Yorker	Bellevedere, IL

DODGE

Caravan	Windsor, Ontario, Canada
Colt	Japan (by Mitsubishi)
Daytona	St. Louis, MO
Dynasty	Bellvedere, IL
Omni	Detroit, MI/Toledo, OH
Shadow	Sterling Hts., MI
Spirit	Newark, NJ/Delaware
Stealth	Japan (by Mitsubishi)

PLYMOUTH

Acclaim	Newark, DE
Colt	Made in Japan by Mitsubishi
Horizon	Detroit, MI/Toledo, OH
Laser	Made in Japan by Mitsubishi and in Normal, IL by Mitsubishi
Sundance	Sterling Hts., MI
Voyager	Windsor, Canada

JEEP

Cherokee, Comanche   Toledo, OH
Wagoneer
Wrangler   Ontario, Canada

CHRYLSER TRUCKS

Dakota   Dodge City, MI
Ram Charger   Alberta, Canada/Mexico
Ram 50   Canada
Ram S10 Pickup   Body made in Canada
                    Engine made by Mitsubishi

EAGLE

Medallion   Made in France by Renault
Monaco   Bramale, Ontario, Canada
Premier   Ontario, Canada
Summit   Made in Japan

GASOLINES

AMERICAN OWNED	FOREIGN OWNED	
Amoco	.	
Atlantic Richfield/Arco	. Boron	England
Chevron	.	
Exxon/Esso	. Gulf	England
Mobil	.	
Phillips 66	. Shell	Netherlands
	. Sohio	England
	. Standard Oil	England
Texaco	. Texaco	Saudi Arabia (refining)
Union 76/Unocal	. Unocal Corp.	Venezuela (refining)
	.	

AUTOMOBILE TIRES

AMERICAN OWNED	FOREIGN OWNED	
Cooper Tire & Rubber .		
(private label tires) .	Alliance Tire	Israel
.	Armstrong	Italy
.	BFGoodrich	France
.	Bridgestone	Japan
.	Continental	Germany
.	Dunlop	Japan
.	Firestone	Japan
Goodyear .		
Kelly Springfield .	General Tire/Gencorp	Germany
.	Michelin	France
.	Mohawk Rubber	Japan
.	Pirelli	Italy
.	Uniroyal	France

Foreign money does not generate jobs or reduce imports. Foreign "transplant" automakers use fewer workers and import more than ten times as many parts as American-owned automakers.

A study by the United Auto Workers estimated that more than half a million jobs have been eliminated as a result of the "transplant" manufacturers. One-third of all foreign autos sold in the United States are "transplants" and not counted as imports.

"Transplants" cost less to produce - up to $700 per car - because of tax breaks and subsidies offered to foreign manufacturers but rarely offered to American manufacturers. Those subsidies were paid for by federal and state taxes.

AIR CARGO

MOVERS

BICYCLES

	. Bianchi USA	Italy
	. (made in Taiwan)	
Burley Tandem	. Bridgestone Cycles	Japan
Cannondale	. Centurion	Japan
(made in USA)	.	
Columbia All Terrain	. Cinelli	Italy
	. Cycles Peugeot USA	France
Diamond Back	. Excel Sports	Italy
(made Taiwan/Jpn)	.	
Fisher Mountain Bikes	. Fuji America	Japan
(made in Taiwan)	.	
GT (Mt. Shasta)	. Giant	Taiwan
Huffy (made in USA)	. Giordana	Italy
Ibis Cycles	.	
Kestrel (made in USA)	. KHS International	Taiwan
Klein Bicycle	.	
Marin Mountain Bikes	. Marinoni	Canada
(made in Taiwan)	.	
Mongoose	. Miele	Canada
Muddy Fox	. Miyata	Japan
(made inTaiwan)	. Motobecane	France
	. Nishiki	Japan
	. Novara	Japan
	. Panasonic	Japan
	. Pinarello	Italy
Ritchey USA	. Raleigh Cycle	England
Road Master	.	
Ross Bicycles USA	. Rocky Mountain	Canada
(made inTaiwan)	.	
Schwinn	.	
(made in Taiwan)	.	
Scott	.	
(made In Taiwan)	.	
Serotta	. Shogun	Japan
Specialized Components		
(made in Taiwan)	.	
Stowe Cycles	.	
(made in USA)	.	

Spectrum   .
   (made in USA)   .
Trek USA   .   Terry   Japan
   (made in USA)   .
   (frames made   .
      in Taiwan)   .   Yokota Cycles USA   Japan

MOTORCYCLES

AMERICAN OWNED   **FOREIGN OWNED**

                        . BMW   Germany
Harley Davidson   . Honda   Japan
                        . Husky/Husqvarna   Italy
                        . Husaberg   Sweden
                        . Kawasaki   Japan
                        . KTM   Austria
                        . Suzuki   Japan
                        . Yamaha   Japan

In 1987, Toyota built an auto assembly plant in Georgetown, Kentucky. Toyota was given 1,500 acres of free land.

The plant was constructed by Ohbayashi Gumi Corporation of Japan using Japanese steel.

Topy Industries of Japan established a wheel factory in nearby Frankfort, Kentucky.

Trinity Industry of Japan opened an auto painting facility in Georgetown.

Five auto parts suppliers set up operations in that area.

The U.S federal government approved a special trade zone in Kentucky allowing Toyota to receive auto parts from Japan duty-free.

Financing was handled by Mitsui Bank of Japan.

United States federal and state government grants and incentives totaled more than $100 million, paid for by federal and state taxes.

Ninety thousand people from 120 countries applied for the 3,000 job openings.

Chapter 3

COMMUNICATIONS & ELECTRONICS

TELEVISION

The future of the video broadcast industry will be high-definition (HDTV), which provides a sharper video image. Among the companies competing to develop worldwide HDTV transmission standards are NHK, the Japan Broadcasting System; a consortium that includes France's Thomson, and Philips of the Netherlands; and Zenith, the last American-owned TV manufacturer, in partnership with AT&T.

Whoever the FCC chooses could dominate HDTV and almost certainly the high-technology industries for the 21st century.

AMERICAN OWNED	FOREIGN OWNED	
	. Casio	Japan
	. Citizen	Japan
	. Cormark	France
	. Fisher	Japan
	. GE/General Electric	France
	. Hitachi	Japan
	. Goldstar	Korea
	. Grundig	Germany
	. Hitachi	Japan
	. JVC	Japan
	. Kenwood USA	Japan
	. Lucky	Korea
	. Magnavox	Netherlands
	. Matsushita	Japan
	. MGA	Japan
	. Mitsubishi	Japan
	. National	Japan
	. NEC	Japan
	. Panasonic	Japan
	. Philco	Netherlands

. Pioneer		Japan
. Proton		Taiwan
. Quasar		Japan
. RCA		France
. Sampo		Taiwan
. Samsung		Korea
. Sansui		England
. Sanyo		Japan
. Sharp		Japan
. Siemens		Germany
. Sony		Japan
. Sylvania		Netherlands
. Technics		Japan
. Telefunken		France
. Thomson		France
. Toshiba		Japan
. Victor		Japan

Zenith .
(made in Springfield, MO)
(small sets made in Mexico)

TELEVISIONS MADE IN AMERICA

Hitachi
Matsushita
Mitsubishi
Sanyo
Sharp
Sony
Toshiba

VCR

The United States is the leader in research and innovation, but European and Asian electronic manufacturers take our discoveries and beat us in the marketplace. Inventive genius wins Nobel Prizes, but superior production wins market share.

Once a new American technology is introduced, our competitors rush to develop it for market, patenting their refinements and improvements. Fifteen years ago, seven out of ten U.S. patents were awarded to American citizens. Now eight of ten U.S. patents go to foreigners. Japan alone owns 32,000 U.S. patents.

The VCR was invented by an American, yet none are manufactured in America. Transistor radios, color televisions, and camcorders top a long list of products originally created by the U.S. but now dominated by foreign producers.

AMERICAN OWNED   FOREIGN OWNED

.	Canon	Japan
.	Chinon	Japan
.	Fisher	Japan
.	GE/General Electric	France
.	Goldstar	Korea
.	Hitachi	Japan
.	JVC	Japan
.	Lucky	Korea
.	Magnavox	Japan
.	MGA	Japan
.	Minolta	Japan
.	Mitsubishi	Japan
.	NEC	Japan
.	Olympus	Japan
.	Panasonic	Japan
.	Philco	Netherlands
.	Pioneer	Japan
.	Proton	Taiwan
.	Philips	Netherlands
.	Quasar	Japan

Realistic	. RCA	France
(Radio Shack)	.	
(made in Japan)	.	
	. Sampo	Taiwan
	. Samsung	Korea
	. Sansui	England
	. Sanyo	Japan
	. Sharp	Japan
	. Sony	Japan
	. Sylvania	Netherlands
	. TDK	Japan
	. Toshiba	Japan
	. Victor	Japan
Zenith (made in Japan).		

STEREO EQUIPMENT

AMERICAN OWNED	FOREIGN OWNED	
	. Aiwa	Japan
	. Akai	Japan
Bose	.	
Carver	. Clarion	Japan
	. Denon	Japan
	. Fisher	Japan
	. GE/General Electric	France
Hafler	. JCV	Japan
	. Kenwood USA	Japan
	. Luxman	Japan
Marantz	. Magnavox	Netherlands
(made in USA)	.	
	. McIntosh	Japan
	. Nakamichi	Japan
Optimus (Radio Shack).	Onkyo	Japan
	. Panasonic	Japan
	. Philco	Netherlands
	. Pioneer	Japan
	. Proton	Taiwan
Realistic (Radio Shack) .	RCA	France
	. Sansui	England

	.	Sanyo	Japan
	.	Sharp	Japan
Shure Sound Systems	.	Sherwood	Japan
	.	Sony	Japan
	.	Sylvania	Netherlands
	.	Technics	Japan
	.	That's America Inc	Japan
	.	Toshiba	Japan
	.	Teac	Japan
	.	Victor	Japan
	.	Yamaha	Japan

CD PLAYERS

AMERICAN OWNED		FOREIGN OWNED	
ADC	.	Aiwa	Japan
	.	Akai	Japan
	.	DBX	England
	.	Denon	Japan
	.	Fisher	Japan
	.	GE/General Electric	France
Hafler	.	Hitachi	Japan
Harmon Kardon/JBL	.	JVC	Japan
	.	Kenwood USA Corp	Japan
	.	Luxman	Japan
Marantz(made in USA)	.	Magnavox	Netherlands
	.	McIntosh	Japan
	.	Nakamichi	Japan
NAD	.	NEC	Japan
	.	Onkyo	Japan
	.	Panasonic	Japan
	.	Philco	Netherlands
	.	Pioneer	Japan
	.	Proton	Taiwan
Realistic (Radio Shack)	.	RCA	France
(made in Japan)	.		
	.	Sansui	England
	.	Sanyo	Japan
	.	Sherwood	Japan

. Sony	Japan
. Sylvania	Netherlands
. Teac	Japan
. Technics	Japan
. Toshiba	Japan
. Yamaha	Japan

RADIO AND TAPE RECORDERS

AMERICAN OWNED	FOREIGN OWNED	
	. Aiwa	Japan
	. Akai	Japan
	. Clarion	Japan
	. Denon	Japan
	. Fisher	Japan
	. GE/General Electric	France
	. JVC	Japan
	. Kenwood USA	Japan
	. Luxman	Japan
Marantz	. Nakamichi	Japan
(made in USA)	.	
NAD	. Onkyo	Japan
	. Panasonic	Japan
	. Philco	Netherlands
	. Pioneer	Japan
	. Proton	Taiwan
	. Quasar	Japan
Realistic (Radio Shack) .		
(some made in USA) .		
	. Sansui	England
	. Sanyo	Japan
	. Seiko	Japan
	. Sherwood	Japan
	. Sony	Japan
	. Teac	Japan
	. Technics	Japan
	. That's America Inc	Japan
	. Toshiba	Japan
	. Yamaha	Japan

AUDIO TAPES

AMERICAN OWNED	FOREIGN OWNED	
	. Afga	Germany
	. BASF	Germany
Centron	. Denon	Japan
(made in Mexico)	.	
	. Fuji	Japan
	. JVC	Japan
Loran	. Maxell	Japan
	. Memorex	England
	. Nakamichi	Japan
	. Philips	Netherlands
Realistic (Radio Shack)	. Sony	Japan
Scotch	. TDK	Japan
3M	. That's America Inc	Japan

VIDEO TAPES

AMERICAN OWNED	FOREIGN OWNED	
	. Afga	Germany
	. BASF	Germany
	. Centron	Japan
	. Fuji	Japan
	. GE/General Electric	France
	. JVC	Japan
Kodak (made in Japan)	. Konica	Japan
	. Maxell	Japan
	. Memorex	England
Polaroid	. Panasonic	Japan
Radio Shack	. RCA	France
Scotch	. SKC	Korea
	. Sony	Japan
3M	. TDK	Japan
Zenith	.	

TYPEWRITERS AND WORD PROCESSORS

AMERICAN OWNED		FOREIGN OWNED	
AT&T	.	AB Dick	England
	.	Brother	Japan
	.	Canon	Japan
	.	Casio	Japan
	.	Epson	Japan
IBM	.	Kenwood	Japan
	.	NEC	Japan
Monroe	.	Okidata	Japan
	.	Olivetti	Italy
	.	Olympia/Olympic	Germany
	.	Panasonic	Japan
	.	Royal	Italy
	.	Samsung	Korea
	.	Sharp	Japan
Smith Corona	.	Silver Reed	Japan
Swintec	.		
Tandy (Radio Shack)	.	TA Adler Royal	Italy
Wang Labs	.		
Xerox	.		

COPIERS

AMERICAN OWNED		FOREIGN OWNED	
	.	AB Dick	England
	.	Adler Royal	Italy
	.	AEG Olympia	Germany
	.	Brother	Japan
	.	Canon	Japan
	.	Fuji	Japan
IBM	.	Gestetner	England
Kodak	.	Konica	Japan
Lanier Worldwide	.	Minolta	Japan
Monroe	.	Mita	Japan
Pitney Bowes	.	Panasonic	Japan

	. Ricoh	Japan
	. Sanyo	Japan
	. Sharp	Japan
	. Toshiba	Japan
Xerox	.	

FACSIMILE EQUIPMENT

AMERICAN OWNED	FOREIGN OWNED	
AT&T	. AEG Olympia/Oly Fax	Germany
	. Brother	Japan
	. Canon	Japan
	. Epson	Japan
	. Fujitsu	Japan
	. Gestetner	England
	. Hitachi	Japan
Lanier Worldwide	. Konica	Japan
	. MITA	Japan
	. Minolta	Japan
Monore	. Murata	Japan
	. NEC/Nefax	Japan
Omnifax	. Olivetti	Italy
	. PanaFax	Japan
Pitney Bowes	. Panasonic	Japan
	. Ricoh	Japan
Swintec	. Samsung	Korea
	. Savin	Netherlands
	. Sharp	Japan
Tandy Fax	. Sony	Japan
(Radio Shack)	. Toshiba	Japan
Xerox	.	

CELLULAR

AMERICAN OWNED	FOREIGN OWNED	
	. Alpine	Japan
	. Diamond Tel	Japan

	.	Ericcson	Sweden
GE/General Electric	.	Fujitsu	Japan
	.	Kenwood Commander	Japan
	.	Matsushita	Japan
Motorola Pulsar	.	Mitsubishi	Japan
	.	NEC America	Japan
	.	Nokia-Mobira	Finland
	.	Novatel	Canada
	.	Oki	Japan
	.	Panasonic	Japan

CAMERAS and FILM

AMERICAN OWNED   FOREIGN OWNED

	.	AGFA Film	Germany
	.	Ansco	Hong Kong
	.	Canon	Japan
	.	Chinon	Japan
	.	Fuji	Japan
	.	Hasselblad	Sweden
Keystone (made USA)	.	Kyocera	Japan
Kodak (made in Asia)	.	Konica	Japan
	.	Leica	Germany
	.	Minolta	Japan
	.	Nikon	Japan
	.	Olympus	Japan
	.	Panasonic	Japan
Polaroid	.	Pentax	Japan
(Some Impulse	.	Ricoh	Japan
cameras are made	.	Rolleiflex	Germany
in USA)	.	Sharp	Japan
	.	Sony	Japan
	.	Vivatar	Australia
	.	Yashica	Japan

CAMCORDERS

AMERICAN OWNED	FOREIGN OWNED	
	. Canon	Japan
	. GE	Japan
	. Hitachi	Japan
	. JVC	Japan
Kodak	. Kyocera	Japan
(made in Japan)	. Magnavox	Japan
	. Matsushita	Japan
	. Minolta	Japan
	. Olympus	Japan
	. Panasonic	Japan
	. Pentax	Japan
	. Philco	Netherlands
	. Quasar	Japan
Realistic (Radio Shack)	. RCA	France
(made in Japan)	. Ricoh	Japan
	. Sharp	Japan
	. Sony	Japan
	. Sylvania	Netherlands
	. Toshiba	Japan
	. Victor	Japan
	. Vivitar	Australia
Zenith (made in Japan) .		

ENTERTAINMENT

FILM STUDIOS:
MOVIE, TELEVISION, VIDEOTAPE

European and Asian electronics companies eagerly entered the entertainment production business for marketing advantages and the potential to influence public opinion. Nine major studios control most of America's movie and TV production, but only four are American-owned. Of the top ten companies that dominate America's music business, only three are American. By producing the movies, TV shows and music that America plays on European and Asian-made VCRs, TV sets and stereo systems, these foreign companies can introduce and sell new advances, such as high-definition television and laser discs, as a package.

Most Americans form their impressions of foreign countries from the media. Foreign investors produce and finance American TV programs, thereby putting themselves in a position to influence what is shown. Viewers must then determine if they are watching entertainment or propaganda.

AMERICAN OWNED	FOREIGN OWNED	
Cannon Pictures	. Carlton Communications	England
Cinemax	. CBS Records/Video	Japan
GTG Entertainment	. Columbia Pictures	Japan
Hanna-Barbera	. Fox Inc	Australia
Hollywood Pictures	.	
Imagine Films	.	
King World Productions	.	
Live Entertainment	. MCA	Japan
Lorimar Telepictures	. MGM/UA	Italy
	. MTM Entertainment	England
Metromedia	. Media Home Entertainment	England
Orion Pictures	. Nelson Entertainment	Canada
Paramount Pictures	. Pathe Communications	Italy
Prism Entertainment	. Qinex Entertainment	Australia
Spelling Entertainment	. RCA Video Productions	Germany

Time Warner	. Technicolor Holdings	England
Touchstone Pictures	. Twentieth Century Fox Film	Australia
Turner Broadcasting	. Tri-Star Pictures	Japan
	. Universal Studios	Japan
Vestron Inc	.	
Viacom International	.	
Walt Disney Studios	.	

RECORDS

AMERICAN OWNED	FOREIGN OWNED	
	. A & M	Netherlands
	. Angel	England
ATCO	. Arista	Germany
Atlantic Records	. Atlanta Artista	Netherlands
	. Big Life	Netherlands
	. Capital Records	England
Concord	. CBS Records	Japan
	. China	Netherlands
	. Chrysalis	Japan/England
	. Columbia Records	Japan
	. Desire	Netherlands
	. Deutshe Grammophon	Netherlands
	. DGC	Japan
Elektra	. ECM	Netherlands
	. EMI Records	England
	. Enigma Records	England
	. Epic	Japan
Fantasy Berkely	. Fiction	Netherlands
	. Fontana	Netherlands
GRP Records	. Geffen Records	Japan
Hollywood Records	. Island Records	Netherlands
K-Tel	. London	Netherlands
MCC/Motown	. Media Records	Netherlands
	. Mercury	Netherlands
	. Mika	Netherlands
	. Philips	Netherlands
	. Polydor	Netherlands
	. Polygram Records	Netherlands

Relativity Records	.	RA	Netherlands
Rhino	.	RCA Records	Germany
Rounder	.	Reckless Records	England
Ryko	.	Rooart	Netherlands
Sire	.	Squawk	Netherlands
	.	TEAC Records	Japan
	.	Thorn/EMI	England
	.	Threshold	Netherlands
Vanguard	.	Vertigo	Netherlands
	.	Verv	Netherlands
	.	Verv Forecast	**Netherlands**
Warner	.		
Communications	.		
WEA Records	.		

MAGAZINES

AMERICAN OWNED		FOREIGN OWNED	
American Health	.	American Baby	England
	.	American Photo	France
	.	(was American Photographer)	
Atlantic	.	Audio	France
Automobile	.		
Aviation Week	.		
Better Homes and	.		
Gardens	.		
Bon Appetite	.	Boat	France
Bride's	.		
Business Week	.		
Byte	.		
Connoisseur	.	Car and Driver	France
Cosmopolitan	.	Computer Hotline	England
Country Home	.		
Magazine	.		
Country Living	.	Cycle World	France
Discover	.	Digital Review	England
Entertainment Weekly	.	ELLE	France
	.	Esquire	England
Family Circle	.		

Field & Stream	.	
Food & Wine	.	
Forbes	.	
Fortune	.	
GQ	.	
Glamour	. Globe	England
Golf Digest	.	
Golf World	.	
Good Housekeeping	.	
Gourmet	.	
Harpers Bazaar	.	
Health	. Health Kids	England
HG/House & Garden	. House Plans	England
House Beautiful	.	
In Health	. In Fashion	Australia
	. Interior Design	England
Ladies Home Journal	.	
Lear	.	
Life	.	
Mademoiselle	.	
McCall's	.	
Metropolitan Home	. Men's Life	Australia
Modern Romance	. Mirabella	Australia
Money Magazine	. Modern Bride	England
	. Mother Earth News	England
	. Motor Boat	England
Muscle & Fitness	. Motor Yacht Intl	England
National Enquirer	. National Examiner	England
New Woman	.	
New York	.	
Newsweek	.	
New Yorker	.	
Outdoor Life	.	
Penthouse	.	
People	. Parade Magazine	England
Playboy	. Parents Magazine	Germany
Popular Mechanics	. Popular Photography	France
Popular Science	. Power & Motor Yacht	France
Premiere	.	
	. Psychology Today	England
Readers Digest	. Racing Times	England
RedBook	.	

Rolling Stone	.	Road & Tack	France
Runner's World/Runner.			
Sassy	.	Sail	England
Self	.		
Seventeen	.		
Soap Opera Digest	.	Smart	England
Soap Opera Weekly	.		
Sports Afield	.	Sound & Image	France
Sports Illustrated	.	Sun	England
Star	.		
Sunset	.		
Teen Beat	.		
Tennis	.		
Time	.		
Town & Country	.		
Travel and Leisure	.		
Travel Holiday	.		
True Romance	.	TV Guide	Australia
True Story	.		
US	.		
US News &	.		
World Report	.		
Vanity Fair	.	Variety	England
Vogue	.		
Weight Watchers	.	Western Sportsman	Canada
Working Woman	.	Woman's Day	France
	.	Your Prom	England

FOREIGN OWNED NEWSPAPERS
(CANADIAN OWNED UNLESS NOTED)

ALABAMA

Dothan	The Dothan Eagle
Enterprise	Enterprise Ledger
Opelika	Opelika-Auburn News

ARIZONA

Globe	Arizona Silver Belt
	Gila Country Shopper

ARKANSAS

Fayetteville	Northwest Arkansas Times
Herber Springs	Cleburne County Times
	Herber Springs Sun
Newport	Bargin Hunters Guide
	Newport Independent

CALIFORNIA

Barstow	Desert Dispatch
Eureka	Siskiyou Daily News
	Times Standard
Oxnard	The Press Courier
Pasadena	Star News
Sacramento	Sacramento Union (owned by South Africa)
West Covina	San Gabriel Valley Daily Tribune
Whittier	The Daily News

COLORADO

Akron	News Reporter
Brush	The Brush News Tribune
Fort Morgan	Morgan Times Review
Julesberg	The Advocate
LaMar	The News
	Tri-State Trader
Sterling	The Journal Advocate
	North Eastern Colorado

CONNECTICUT

Ansonia	The Evening Sentinel
Bridgeport	The Bridgeport Post
	The Telegram
Naugatuck	Naugatuck Daily News

FLORIDA

Key West	The Key West Citizen
Marianna	Jackson County Floridan
New Smyrna Beach	News and Observer
Orange Park	Clay Today

GEORGIA

Americus	Americus Times-Recorder
Cordele	The Cordele Dispatch
Dalton	The Daily Citizen-News
Griffin	Griffin Daily News
Tifton	The Tifton Gazette
Valdosta	The Valdosta Daily Times

HAWAII

Oahu	Honolulu Pennysaver
	Leeward Pennysaver
	Waikiki Pennysaver
	Windward Pennysaver

IDAHO

Blackfoot	The Morning News

ILLINOIS

Albion	Albion Journal
	Prairie Post
Benton	Benton Evening News
Canton	Canton Daily News
	The Little Giant Shopper
Carmi	The Carmi Times
	White County Shopper News
Carmi/El Dorado	The Spectator
Chester	Chester Herald Tribune
	The Chester Shopper
Christopher	Christopher Free Press
	Christopher Progress
DuQuoin	DuQuoin Evening Call
El Dorado	El Dorado Daily Journal
	Weekender
Flora	Clay Country Advocate
Galatia	The Money Stretcher
Galesburg	Knox Pennysaver
Grayville	Mercury Independent
Harrisburg	The Daily Register
Herrin	Herrin Spokesman
Jacksonville	Jacksonville Journal Courier
Marion	Buyers Guide
	The Homemaker
	The Marion Daily Republican
Monmouth	Consumer Focus
	Henderson County Pennysaver
	Ogwaka Current
	Review-Atlas
Mount Vernon	Register-News
Murphysboro	Buyers Guide
	Murphysboro American
Norris City	The Banner
Olney	The Daily Mail
	The Yellow Sheet

ShawneeTown	Gallatin Democrat
	Ridgeway News
Sterling	The Daily Gazette
	Sterling Rock Falls Daily Gazette
West Frankfort	Buyers Guide
	The Daily American
White County	The Money Saver

INDIANA

Anderson	Anderson Herald-Bulletin
Batesville	Herald-Tribune
Columbia City	The Post and Mail
Decatur	Decatur Daily Democrat
	Monroeville News
Greensburg	The Greensburg Daily News
Hartford City	Hartford City News-Times
	The Market Basket
Kokomo	The Kokomo Tribune
New Albany	The Tribune
Rensselaer	The Republican
Rushville	Rushville Republican
Terre Haute	The Tribune Star
Valparaiso	The Vidette-Messenger

IOWA

Atlantic	Atlantic News-Telegraph
	Atlantic Times
	Good Sense Shopper
Charles City	Charles City Press
	Six County Shopper
	The Look and Shop
Council Bluffs	The Daily Nonpareil
Oelwein	Oelwein Daily Register

KANSAS

Atchinson	Atchinson Daily Globe
Augusta	The Advertiser
	The Daily Gazette
	The Daily Reporter
	The Daily Reporter Plus
	Market Corner
	Shoppers Guide
	The Times
	McPherson Sentinel
Leavenworth	The Leavenworth Times

KENTUCKY

Corbin	Corbin Times Tribune
Richmond	The Richmond Register

LOUISIANA

Lafayette	The Daily Advertiser

MARYLAND

Cumberland	Cumberland, Maryland Times/News
Dickinson	The Dickinson Press
Salisbury	The Daily Times

MASSACHUSETTS

Boston	Boston Herald (owned by Australia)
Fitchburg	Sentinel and Enterprise
North Adams	The Transcript
Taunton	Taunton Daily Gazette

MICHIGAN

Adrian	The Daily Telegram
Benton Harbor	The Herald Palladium
Cheboygan	The Cheboygan Daily Tribune
	The Northern Advertiser
	The Shoppers Fair

Escanaba	The Daily Press
Houghton	The Daily Mining Gazette
Ionia	Sentinel Standard
Iron Mountain	The Daily News
Marquette	The Mining Journal
Sault Ste. Marie	The County Buyers Guide
	The Evening News
South Haven	South Haven Daily Tribune

MINNESOTA

Albert Lea	The Albert Lea Evening Tribune
Austin	Austin Daily Herald
Crookston	The Times
	The Valley Shopper
Fergus Falls	The Daily Journal
Stillwater	The Gazette
	Midweek
Worthington	Worthington Daily Globe

MISSISSIPPI

Kosciusko	Kosciusko Star Herald
Laurel	Laurel Leader-Call
Pontotoc	Pontotoc Progress

MISSOURI

Boonville	The Record
	Boonville Daily News
Camdenton	Good News Shopper
	Reveille
Carthage	The Carthage Press
Caruthersville	Bootheel Beacon
	Democrat Angus
	Missouri Herald
	Pemiscot Journal
Chillicothe	Constitution Tribune
Farmington	Farmington Press Advertiser
Fredericktown	Democrat News
Greenfield	Greenfield Vedette
	Lake Stockton Shopper

Hannibal	Mark Twain Shopper
Keytesville	Chariton Courier
Lanagan	Big Nickel
Macon	Chronicle-Herald
	The Journal
Malden	Press Merit
	The Delta News
Marcelini	Marcelini Press
Mexico	The Mexico Ledger
Miller	Miller Press
Monroe City	Monroe City News
Neosho	Neosho Daily News
Osaga Beach	Lake Sun Beach
Rolla	Rolla Area Sun
	Rolla Daily News
Salem	Salem Area Sun
Sedalia	The Sedalia Democrat
Sikeston	The Democrat Standard
St. James	St. James Leader Journal
	The Advertiser
Trumann	Trumann Democrat
Waynesville	The Daily Fort Gateway Guide
	The Pulaski County Sun

NEBRASKA

Sidney	Sidney Telegraph Shopper

NEW HAMPSHIRE

Portsmouth	The Portsmouth Herald

NEW JERSEY

Bridgeton	Bridgeton Evening News

NEW YORK

Bath	The Steuben Courier
Dansville	Genesee County Express
Herkimer	The Evening Telegram

Hornell	The Evening Tribune
	The Spectator
	The Tribune Extra
Newburgh	The Evening News
New York City	New York Daily News (England)
North Tonawanda	The Record Advertiser
	Tonawanda News
Olean	The Independent Olean Press
	Times Herald
Oswego	The Palladium Times
Penn Van	Chronicle Express
	The Chronical Advertiser
Salamanca	The Penny Saver
	Salamanca Republican
Wellsville	The Reporter Plus
	Wellsville Pennysaver
	Wellsville Reporter

NORTH CAROLINA

Elizabeth City	The Daily Advance
Monroe	The Enquirer-Journal
Rocky Mount	The Evening Telegram
Shelby	The Shelby Star

NORTH DAKOTA

Grand Forks	New Tri-County Press
Jamestown	Jamestown Sun
	Sun Country
	The Prairie Post

OHIO

Ashtabula	The Star Beacon
Canton	The Repository
Chardon	The Geauga Times Leader
Conneaut	The News Herald
Coshocton	The Coshocton Tribune
East Liverpool	The Evening Review
Greenville	The Daily Advocate
Hamilton	The Journal News

Lancaster	Jacksonville Journal Courier
Mansfield	News Journal
Marion	The Marion Star
Middletown	Middletown Journal
Minster	The Community Post
Newark	The Advocate
Piqua	Piqua Daily Call
Portsmouth	The Portsmouth Daily Times
Salem	The Salem News
St. Mary's	The Evening Leader
Steubenville	The Herald Star
Wapakoneta	Auglaize Merchandiser
	Shawnee-Cridersville Press
	Shelby-Auglaize Review
	Wapakoneta Daily News
Warren	The Tribune Chronicle
Xenia	The Xenia Daily Gazette
Zanesville	The Times Recorder

OKLAHOMA

Ada	The Ada Evening News
Enid	Enid Morning News & Eagle
Woodward	The Phoenix
	The Shopper
	Woodward News

PENNSYLVANIA

Altoona	Altoona Mirror
Bradford	The Bradford Era
Brockway	The Brockway Record
Connellsville	The Daily Courier
Corry	Corry Journal
Easton	The Express
Everett	The Shopper Guide
Greenville	Greenville Record-Argus
Hanover	The Evening Sun
Kane	The Kane Republican
Kittanning	The Leader Times
Lebanon	The Daily News
Lock Haven	The Express

Meadville	The Meadville Tribune
Monessen	The Valley Independent
New Castle	New Castle News
Punxsutawney	Spirit Extra
Reynoldsville	The Reynoldsville Star
Ridgeway	The Ridgeway Record
	Shoprite
Sayre	Sayre Evening Times
Shamokin	The News Item
St. Mary's	The Daily Press
Sykesville	The Sykesville Post Dispatch
Titusville	Titusville Herrald
Waynesboro	The Record Herald
Youngsville	Warren County Buyers Guide

SOUTH CAROLINA

Florence	Florence Morning News

SOUTH DAKOTA

Mitchell	The Mexico Ledger

TENNESSEE

Crossville	Crossville Chronicla
	Cumberland Times

TEXAS

Big Spring	Big Spring Herald
Del Rio	Del Rio News Herald
Huntsville	The Huntsville Item
Kerrville	Kerrville Daily News
Marshall	Marshall News Messenger
San Antonio	San Antonio Express News (Australia)
San Marcos	The Daily Record
	Hill Country Shoppers Guide

UTAH

St. George   The Daily Spectrum

VIRGINIA

Petersburg   The Progress Index

WEST VIRGINIA

Beckley	The Register Herald
Bluefield	Bluefield Daily Telegram
Charleston	Charleston Daily Mail
Fairmont	The Times West Virginia
Oak Hill	The Fayette Tribune
Weirton	The Weirton Daily Times

WISCONSIN

Appleton	The Bulletin
	The Post-Crescent
Fond du Lac	Fond du Lac Reporter
Manitowoc	Herald Times Reporter
	News Journal
Oconomowoc	Oconomowoc Enterprise
Sheboygan	The Sheboygan Press
Waukesha	Waukesha County Freeman
West Bend	West Bend News
Wisconsin Rapids	The Daily Tribune

BOOK PUBLISHERS/IMPRINTS

AMERICAN OWNED	FOREIGN OWNED	
Alfred A. Knopf	. American Publishing	Canada
Avon Books	. Argus Press	England
Ballentine	. B. Dalton	Netherlands
Berkley	. Ballinger	Netherlands
Berkshire Hathaway	. Bantum	Germany
	. Barnes & Noble	Netherlands
	. Basic Books Inc	Australia
	. Bertlesmann AG	Germany
	. Bradbury Press	England
	. Camden House	Canada
	. Cardiff	England
Charter	. Carlton Communications	England
Crown	. Cordura Corp	Canada
	. (Los Angeles, CA)	
Dekker Marcel Inc	. Delacorte Press	Germany
DelRay	. Dell	Germany
R.R. Donnelley & Sons	. Diamandis	France
Dow Jones	. Doubleday	Germany
Dun & Bradstreet	. E. P. Dutton	England
Farrar Straus &	. Faber & Faber	England
Girous	.	
Fawcett	. FourWinds Press	England
Fireside Paperbacks	. The Free Press	England
Grove	. GoldEagle	Canada
	. Gordon	Netherlands
	. Grolier Press	France
	. Gruner & Jahr	Germany
	. Hachette	France
	. Harlequin Books	Canada
Houghton Mifflin Co	. Harper Collins	Australia
	. (was Harper & Row)	
Ivy	. Haynes	England
Jove	.	
Knightsbridge	.	
Publishing	.	
Lane	. Lexicon	Korea
Little & Brown	. J. B. Lippincott	Netherlands

McGraw Hill	. Maxwell/MacMillan	England
	. Mentor	England
	. Meridian	England
	. Merrill	England
William Morrow & Co	.	
	. New American Library	England
W. W. Norton	.	
	. Octopus Books	England
	. Onyx	England
	. Penguin Publishing	England
Pantheon	. Perennial Library	Australia
Pocket	. Pergamon Press	Lichtenstein
Prentice Hall	. Plume	England
Price Stern Sloan	. Praeger	Netherlands
Putnam	.	
Quill	.	
Random House	. Raven Press	Netherlands
Reader's Digest	. Reed International	England
Rodale Press	. Regents Publishers	Korea
Sceptre Books	.	
E. W. Scripps	. St. Martin's Press	England
Serendipity Books	. Salem House	Australia
	. Scarecrow Press	Korea
	. Signet	England
Simon & Schuster	. Springhouse	Netherlands
Summit	. Silhouette Books	Canada
Tab/Liberty House	. Torchbooks	Australia
Time-Life	. Torstar Books	Canada
Troubador Press	. Triangle	Australia
	. Van Nostrand Reinhold	Canada
Villard	. Viking Press	England
Western Publishing	. Worldwide Library	Canada
	. York Press	Canada
Zebra Books	. Zondervan	Australia

The American consumer-electronics industry was born in an explosion of creativity and innovation but died prematurely in a fatal attempt to boost profits by moving production offshore and by licensing its technology. Lured by cheaper labor, American manufacturers moved assembly plants to Third World countries. Soon component manufacuring followed, and then the production of whole systems. Once research and development moved out of the United States, it left only a "hollow corporation" that imported and relabeled finished goods - sometimes made by its former competitors. For instance, Kodak sells Cannon photocopies, Matsushita video cameras and TDK tapes - - all labeled "Kodak".

In an effort to tap closed foreign markets, U.S. manufacturers sold (or sometimes gave) details of electronic inventions to foreign producers, who then manufactured and sold these products back at less than cost. This practice, known as "dumping," continued until that American industry went out of business. In 1955, America manufactured 96% of all radios sold, but by the late 80s, almost none In 1968, 28 American TV manufacturers dominated the industry. Less than two decades later, only one American-owned television manufacturer, Zenith, remained, holding 12% of the American market.

Chapter 4

COMPUTERS

COMPUTER HARDWARE

When the Computer Age began, America produced 94% of all computers sold. Today, it is closer to half, and all the key technology for laptops - batteries, disk drives, and screens - are produced in Asia.

AMERICAN OWNED

FOREIGN OWNED

	. Acer America	Taiwan
	. Advanced Logic	40% Singapore
	. Research/ARC	
	. Altos Computer	Taiwan
	. American Research Corp/ARC	Taiwan
	. Amiga	Bahamas
Apple	. Amstrad	England
Arche Technologies	. Apricot Computers	England
AST Research	. Ardent Computers	Japan
AT&T	. Blue Chip	Japan
	. Brother	Japan
	. Bull	France
	. C3 Inc	England
	. C. Itoh	Japan
	. Canon	Japan
	. Casio	Japan
	. CEI Systems	Japan
	. Chinon	Japan
	. Citizen	Japan
Compaq	. Comark	France
	. Computor/Amiga	Bahamas
	. Computor Power Group	Australia
	. Computor Systems Devlpmnt	England
	. Cordata Technologies	Korea
Data General	. Data Tech Enterprises	Taiwan
Datavue	. Datatronics	Sweden
DEC/Digital Equip.Co.	. Display Components/TDK	Japan

Dell Computers Corp	.	
Emerson	. Epson	Japan
(made in Japan)	.	
Excel	. Everex Systems	Hong Kong
	. Fujitsu	Japan
	. Goldstar	Korea
	. Gould	Japan
Grid Systems	. Groupe Bull/Honeywell	France
HewlettPackard/Apollo	. Headstart/Vendex	Netherlands
	. Hitachi	Japan
	. Hyundai	Korea
IBM	. ICL	England
	. Intelligent Storage	Japan
Laser	. Leading Edge	Korea
	. Logitec	Swiss
	. Magnovox	Netherlands
	. Matra	France
	. Matsushita	Japan
	. MBP	Germany
	. Memorex Telex	Netherlands
	. Microfocus	England
	. Microsystems Group	England
	. Minolta	Japan
	. Mitac	Taiwan
	. MIPS Systems	Japan
Mohawk Qantel	. Mitsubishi	Japan
	. National Advanced Systems	Japan
	. NEC	Japan
	. Nixdorf/Siemens	Germany
	. Normerel	France
Northgate Computors	. NorthAmerican Philips	Netherlands
	. Norelco	Netherlands
	. Okodata	Japan
Omega Systems	. Olivetti	Italy
Packard Bell	. Panasonic	Japan
	. Philips	Netherlands
	. Plessey	England
	. Poqet	Japan
	. Psion	England
Qantel/Mohawk	.	
Smith Corona	. Ricoh	Japan

Sun Microsystems	. Samsung	Korea
	. Sanyo	Japan
	. SGS	Italy/France
	. Seiko	Japan
	. Sentel	England
	. Sharp	Japan
	. Sony	Japan
	. Suntel Computers	England
Tandem Computers	.	
Tandon	.	
Tandy	. TDK Display	Japan
Texas Instruments	. Thomson	France
	. Toshiba	Japan
Ultimate Corp	. Vendex/Headstart	Netherlands
Wang	. Wyse Technology	Taiwan
Xerox	. Xetel Corp	Japan
	. Zenith Computors	France

"Nations do not have permanent enemies; nor do they have permanent friends."

Henry John Temple

Shintaro Ishihara, in his book, *The Japan That Can Say No*, boasts that Americans are reaching the point where "if Japan stopped selling them chips, there would be nothing they could do." Indeed, twenty-one critical military systems contain foreign-made chips, and there are many foreign-made chips in the F-16 fighter and other advanced weapons. Nearly half of the high-tech weaponry used in Desert Storm in Iraq was not made in the United States. Although based on U.S. technology, it was produced by our foreign competitors.

COMPUTOR SOFTWARE

AMERICAN OWNED   FOREIGN OWNED

Adobe Systems/   .
  Postscript   .
Alpha Systems Sftwre .
Ashton Tate   . Applied Information Software Australia
Auto Desk   .
Beagle Brothers   .
Bloc Development   .
Borland   . Boston Software Publishers   Swiss
Broderbond   .
Cambridge Software   .
Central Point/PC Tools .
Clarion   .
Claris (Apple)   .
Computer Associates   . Computor Services Corp.   Japan
                             . Cornell Computor Corp.   Australia
                             . Cullinet Software   Swiss
DAC Easy Software   . DAI Decisions Systems   England
DataLogic Software   . Data Architects Systems   England
Datasoft/Software   .
  Toolworks   .
DEC Software   .
Easy Soft   .
Fifth Generation   .
Format Software   .
Fox Software   .
                             . Goal Systems Software   France
                             . Grolier Publishing   France
Informix Software   .
Intuit   .
Lotus   . Logitech   Swiss
Matrix Software   . MBP   Germany
Micro Logic   .
Microsoft   .
Novell   .
Oracle Software   .
Peachtree Software   .
Phoenix Technologies .

Pisces Software	. Program Systems	New Zealand
Reference Software	.	
Quick Soft Inc./	.	
PC Write	.	
	. RightSoft Inc./Rightwriter	England
Software Toolworks	. I.P. Sharp	Canada
Software Products Intl.	. Sphere Software	England
Spinnacker Software	. Software AG Systems	Germany
Symantec	.	
Tandy	. Tindall Associates	Swiss
	. Tomcat Computor Corp.	Japan
WordPerfect	. Wolters Samson	Netherlands
Z Soft Corp.	. Zortech	England

America appears to be driven by a short-term philosophy. It's been said that while our foreign competitors look ten years ahead, we look ten minutes ahead. We don't even buy green bananas. But America's short-term mindset is not due to cultural preference but rather to the cost of our capital. In 1985, our capital cost almost 10%, compared to less than 6% in Japan. On a fifteen-year project, the United States would pay 69% more in total interest. One of the factors that determine cost of capital is savings, and America's savings rate is only 5% while Japan's is three times that rate. Korea's rate is 20% and Taiwan's, more than 30%.

Chapter 5

BANKS AND INSURANCE

The United States government has complex and often confusing regulations that restrict the growth and expansion of U.S.-owned banks. These regulations do not apply to foreign banks, which, in effect, operate in a deregulated environment giving them a competitive advantage.

BANKS AND FINANCIAL SERVICES

The World's 25 Largest Banks

1. Dai-Ichi Kangyo Bank (Japan)
2. Mitsui Taiyo Kobe Bank (Japan)
3. Sumitomo Bank (Japan)
4. Fuji Bank (Japan)
5. Mitsubishi Bank (Japan)
6. Sanwa Bank (Japan)
7. Credit Agricole (France)
8. Industrial Bank of Japan (Japan)
9. Banque Nationale de Paris (France)
10. Credit Lyonnais (France)
11. Deutsche Bank (Germany)
12. Tokai Bank (Japan)
13. Norinchukin Bank (Japan)
14. Mitsubishi Trust & Banking (Japan)
15. Sumitomo Trust & Banking (Japan)
16. Barclays (U.K.)
17. ABN AMRO Holdings (Netherlands)
18. Bank of Tokyo (Japan)
19. Societe Generale de France (France)
20. Mitsui Trust & Banking (Japan)
21. Long-Term Credit Bank of Japan (Japan)
22. Citicorp (U.S.)
23. Yasuda Trust & Banking (Japan)
24. National Westminster Bank (U.K.)
25. Dresdner Bank (Germany)

AMERICAN OWNED	FOREIGN OWNED	
H. F. Ahmanson Corp .	Allied Finance Co (Dallas TX)	Swiss
Ameritrust .	Atlantic Bank (New York)	Greece
Banc One Corp .	Bank of California	Japan
.	400 California, San Francisco	
.	45 Wall Street, New York	
.	550 S. Flower, Los Angeles	
.	800 Wilshire Blvd., Los Angeles	
BankAmerica .		
(Security Pacific) .		
Bank of Boston .	Bank of Honolulu	Indonesia
Bancorp Hawaii .		
Bank of New England .	Bank of New England	Japan
.	Leasing Unit	
Bank of New York .	Bank of Palm Springs	Japan
Bankers Trust NewYork .	Bank of The West	France
Barnett Banks .	Barclays Group	England
Bay Banks (Boston) .	Bay Financial Corp (Boston)	England
Boatmens Bancshares .	Boston SafeDeposit & Trust	Japan
CalFed Inc/ .	California First Bank	Japan
California Fed. Bank .	(Los Angeles/San Diego/Portland)	
Chase Manhattan .	California First of San Francisco	Japan
Chemical Banking .	Centrust Savings Bank	Saudi Arabia
(Manufactuers .	(Florida)	
Hanover) .		
Citicorp .	Chicago Harris Bank	Canada
Citizens & Southern .	CIT Group Inc	Japan
Comerica .	Crocker National Bank of	England
.	San Francisco	
Continental Bank Corp .	CS Bank of Boston	Swiss
CoreStates Financial/ .		
Philadelphia National/ .		
First Pennsylvania .		
Crestar Financial .		
CrossLand Savings .		
Dime Savings Bank .		
Dominion Bank of VA. .	El Camino Bank	Australia
First Bank System .	FarWest Financial Corp	Canada

First Chicago Corp	Financial Collection Agency — Canada
(Saudi Arabia 7.6%).	(AZ, CO, CT, DE, FL, GA, IL, IN, LA,
	MI, MN, MO, NC, NJ, NV, NY, OH,
	OK, PA, SC, TX, VA, WA, WI)
First City Bancorp	First American Bank — Netherlands
of Texas	Silver Springs, MD/New York, NY/
	McLean, VA/Washington DC
First Fidelity Bancorp	First American Metro Corp — Netherlands
First Hawaiian	(Virginia)
First Interstate	First Boston Group — Swiss
Bancorp	
First of America Bank	First City Credit Co — Canada
First Union National	(Seattle, WA)
First Virginia Bank	
First Wachovia	First City Financial (New York) Canada
	First City Securities (Nevada) Canada
	First Colonial Bank (Chicgo) Netherlands/
	Antilles
	First Federal of Rochester (NY) Canada
	First International S & L — Japan
	First Jersey National — England
	First Los Angeles Bank — Italy
	First Maryland Bancorp — Ireland
	First National Bank Trust — Canada
	(Illinois)
	First NH Banks Inc — Ireland
	First Pennsylvania Corp — Hong Kong
	First State Bank of So.Cal. — Korea
Fleet/Norstar	(Santa Fe Springs, CA)
Financial	
GlenFed/Glendale	
Federal	
Golden West Financial	Global Union Bank — Hong Kong
	(2 New York branches)
Great American Bank	Grolier Credit Services — Korea
Great Western	Harris Bank — Canada
Financial	(Glencoe, IL/ Northbrook, IL/
	Hinsdale, IL/Naperville, IL/
	New York, NY/Roselle, IL/
	Wilmette, IL/Winetka, IL)
	Harris Corp Finance — Canada
	(Chicago)

Hibernia	. Harris Trust & Savings	Canada
(New Orleans)	. (Chicago)	
Home Fed Bank	. Harris Trust Company	Canada
(San Diego)	. (Scottsdale, AZ/San Francisco/	
	. West Palm Beach, FL/New York)	
	. Hoche Financial Inc	France
	. International S&L (Hawaii)	Japan
KeyCorp	. Kidde Credit	England
	. Kleinwort Benson Government	Japan
	. Securities (Chicago)	
	. LaSalle National Bank	Netherlands
	. (Lakeview Bank, Chicago/	
	. LaSalle Bank, Chicago/	
	. Lisle Bank, Northbrook Bank,	
	. NW National Bank, Chicago)	
	. Lloyds Bank US	Japan
	. Manufacturers Hanover	Japan
	. CIT Group	
	. Marine Midland of NY	Hong Kong/Shanghı
Mellon Bank	. Manufacturers Bank	Japan
	. (now Mitsui Manufacturers)	
Meridian Bancorp	. Midland Bank of New York	England
Meritor Savings Bank	.	
Michigan National	.	
Midlantic	.	
MNC Financial/	.	
Maryland Bank	.	
JP Morgan	.	
National City	. National Bank	Denmark
(Cleveland)	.	
NBD Bancorp	. National Bank of Georgia	Netherlands
Nations Bank	.	
(NCNB/C&S Sovran)	.	
Northern Trust	. National Bank of Washington	Saudi Arabia
Norwest	. National Bancshares Corp	Egypt
	. (Texas)	
	. National Westminister	
	. Bank USA	
	. NBG Financial (Atlanta, GA)	Netherlands
	. New London Trust Corp	Canada
	. (New London, NH)	

PNC Financial	. Pacific First Financial	Canada
(Pittsburgh)	. (Washington State)	
Principle Finance	. Pacific Savings Bank	Canada
	. (Southern California)	
	. Republic Financial Services	Swiss
	. (Dallas, TX)	
Republic New York	.	
(29% Swiss)	.	
	. Republic of New York	Luxembourg
	. Royal Trust Co Ltd	Canada
	. Sanwa Bank of California	Japan
Shawmut National	.	
Signet Bank	.	
(15%) Spain	.	
Society Corp	.	
Southeast Banking	.	
SunTrust Banks	.	
State Street (Boston)	. Tilden Financial Corp	England
UJB Financial	. Ultra Bancorp (New Jersey)	England
	. Union Bank (California)	Japan
United Jersey Bank	. United Bank (San Francisco)	Hong Kong
US Bancorp	. Universal Savings Bank	Australia
	. Valley Fidelity Bank & Trust	Netherlands
	. (Knoxville, TN)	
	. Valley National Bank	Italy
	. (Glendale, CA)	
Wells Fargo & Co	. Washington Bank Corp	Netherlands/
	. (Washington, DC)	Antilles
World S & L	. Westchester Financial Services	Hong Kong
	. (New York)	

In 1982, the United States was the world's largest creditor nation.
Three years later, it became a debtor nation and the largest
recipient of foreign investment. Foreign lenders now finance the
bulk of our budget deficit, and foreign investors hold more than
10% of outstanding U.S. treasury bills - enough to wield economic
power and shape national decisions and policy.

Money equals power, and money is rarely neutral for long, as any
former colony can tell you. The gradual transfer of wealth and
power that we are witnessing usually happens on a battlefield.
This time the front line is Wall Street.

INSURANCE

The World's 10 Largest Insurers

1. Nippon Life (Japan)
2. Prudential (U.S.)
3. Zenkyoren (Japan)
4. Dai-Ichi Mutual Life (Japan)
5. Sumitomo Life (Japan)
6. Metropolitan Life (U.S.)
7. Allianz Group (Germany)
8. Union des Assurances des Paris (France)
9. Aetna Life & Casualty (U.S.)
10. Meiji Mutual Life (Japan)

AMERICAN OWNED	FOREIGN OWNED	
Aetna Life & Casualty	Aigon USA	Netherlands
	Agra Benefit	Netherlands
Alexander & Alexander	Albany Insurance Co (NY)	England
Alexander Hamilton	Allied Finance Co (Dallax, TX)	Swiss
Allstate	American Benefit Counselors (Maryland)	Netherlands
American Family Life	American Crown Life	Canada
American Financial Corp	American First Insurance (Tampa, FL)	Netherlands
American General Life	American Guaranty & Liability (Roselle, IL)	Swiss
American Intl. Group	Americas Insurance Co (New Orleans, LA)	England
American Life & Accident	American Old Line Life (South Carolina)	England
American Life of NY		
American National Insurance	Amev Insurance	Netherlands
Aon Corp	Associated Doctors Health Life (Birmingham, AL)	Netherlands
	Associated Life Insurance (Wisconsin)	Canada
	Atlantic Casualty & Fire (Columbus, SC)	Bermuda

5-6

	. Atlas Associates of America	England
	. (NY/NJ)	
Berkshire Hathaway	. Bankers Financed Life (MD)	Netherlands
Insurance	.	
	. Bankers Unifed Life Assurance	Netherlands
	. (Iowa)	
	. Banner Life Insurance	England
	. Better Homes Insurance (IL)	Netherlands
	. Blue Ridge Insurance	Swiss
	. (Dallas, TX)	
	. Brown & Williams	Canada
	. Cadet Corp (Iowa)	Netherlands
	. CalFed Syndicate	England
	. Camden Fire Insurance	Scotland
	. (Philadelphia, PA)	
	. Capital Assurance Life	Netherlands
	. (Denver, CO)	
	. Capital Bankers Life (WI)	Canada
Cenguard	. Central National Insurance	Puerto Rico
Chubb	. (Omaha, NE)	
Cigna Inc	. Clarendon Insurance	Canada
Cluett Peabody Intl	.	
	. Commercial Union	England
	. Confederation Life	Canada
CNA Financial/	. Consolidated Insurance Co	Netherlands
Equicor-Equitable	. (Indianapolis, IN)	
Colonial Penn	. Copa Inc (Iowa)	Netherlands
Connecticut General	.	
Life	. Cosmopolitan American Life	Netherlands
Continental Corp	. (Denver, CO)	
	. Creditor Resources (CA/GA)	Netherlands
	. Cross Country Life (AR)	Netherlands
	. Crown Life Insurance	Canada
	. Crump & Co	England
	. (Atlanta, GA/Dallas, TX/	
	. Hartford, CT)	

Cuna Mutual Insurance.	CUIC Investors	England
.	(Lafayette, CA/Memphis, TN)	
.	Eagle Star Life	England
.	Empire Fire & Marine	Swiss
.	(Omaha, NE)	
.	Employees Fire Insurance	England
.	Equitable Life Assurance	France
.	Society	
.	Equity National Life	Netherlands
.	(Atlanta, GA)	
.	Excelsior Insurance	Netherlands
.	(Syracuse, NY)	
Family Life Insurance .	Farmers Insurance Group	England
.	(Los Angeles)	
.	Farmers Merchants Insurance	England
.	(Tulsa, OK)	
Federal Home .		
Financial Guardian Intl .	Fidelity Southern Insurance	Netherlands
.	(Augusta, GA)	
.	Fidelity Union Life (TX)	Germany
Franklin Life Insurance .	Financial Investors Life (MI)	Netherlands
.	Fire Underwriters	England
.	Fireman's Fund	Germany
.	First of Georgia	Netherlands
.	First Georgia Life	England
.	First Insurance of Hawaii	Japan
.	First RE Life Insurance (MD)	Netherlands
GEICO Corp .	General Accident Fire & Life	Scotland
.	(Pennsylvania)	
Globe Life & Accident .	General Accident	Scotland
Golden State Insurance.	General Casulty Co (WI)	Swiss
General RE Corp .		
Guardian Life Ins .	General Services (Iowa)	Netherlands
Guardsman Life Ins .	Georgia US Corp	Netherlands
Gulf Insurance .	Globe Indemnity Co	England
.	(Charlotte, NC)	
.	Great Western Life	Canada
.	Great West Life Associates	Canada
.	Guardian Royal Exchange	England
Hartford ,	Hawaiian Life Insurance	Japan

Home Insurance Group	. Home Guaranty Ins (VA)	Finland
	. Houston Post Insurance	Canada
	. Indiana Insurance	Netherlands
	. Industrial Life Ins (Dallas, TX)	Swiss
	. Insured Lloyds (Dallas, TX)	Swiss
	. Integrity and National	Australia
	. Integrity Life	
	. Intl Life Investors of NY	Netherlands
	. Investors Security	Netherlands
	. Investors Warranty of America	Netherlands
	. (Georgia)	
	. Iowa Fidelity Life	Netherlands
	. Jackson National Life	England
	. (Dallas, TX/Lansing, MI)	
Jefferson-Pilot	. Fred S. James & Co	England
John Hancock Mutual	.	
Kemper Insurance	.	
Lincoln Natl Corp	. LaBow Haynes Co	England
	. (Nashville, TN)	
Loews Insurance	. Life Investors (Iowa)	Netherlands
	. Life Insurance Co of Georgia	Netherlands
	. Life of Boston	Canada
	. Loyal American Life Insurance	Canada
	. (Mobile, AL)	
	. MacCabees Life	England
Marsh & McLennan	. Maine Fidelity Life	Canada
MassMutual	.	
Metropolitan Life	. Manufacturers Life (MI)	Canada
Monarch Life Ins	. Manufacturers Life Insurance	Canada
	. of America (Pennsylvania)	
Mony Insurance of	. Maryland Casualty Copany	Swiss
Canada	.	
Mutual of Omaha	. Massachusetts Fidelity	Netherlands
Mutual Life of NY	. MB Victoria (Wisconsin)	England
	. Mercantile General of America	England
	. (Morristown, NJ)	
	. Merritt Insurance	Netherlands
	. Mid-America Fire & Casualty	England
	. (Ohio)	
	. Midwestern United Life	Netherlands
	. (Ft Wayne, IN)	
	. Milbank Insurance (SD)	England

	.	Midwestern Life	England
	.	Monumental General (MD)	Netherlands
Nationwide Mutual	.	National Old Line	Netherlands
	.	(Little Rock, AR)	
New England Mutual	.	New American Life	England
Life	.	(Columbia, MO)	
New York Life	.	New Mark Insurance	England
	.	(Charlotte, NC)	
NWNL/Northwestern	.	Nobel Insurance Ltd	Bermuda
Mutual Life	.	(TX/TN/PA)	
	.	North American Life	Canada
	.	Assurance	
	.	North American Life &	Germany
	.	Casualty (Minnesota)	
	.	North American Reassurance	Swiss
	.	North American Security	Canada
	.	Life (Maine)	
	.	North American Specialty	Scotland
	.	(Manchester, NH)	
	.	Northern Assurance of	England
	.	America	
	.	Northwest Life Assurance	Canada
	.	(Washington)	
	.	North Pacific Insurance	Scotland
	.	(Portland, OR)	
	.	NRG America (Philadelphia,PA)	Netherlands
Ohio Casualty	.	Ohio State Life	England
Ohio National Life	.	Oregon Automobile Insurance	Scotland
	.	Pacific Fidelity Life	Netherlands
	.	(Cedar Rapaids, IA)	
	.	Pacific Guardian Life	Japan
Phoenix Mutual Life	.	Peerless Insurance	England
Pilot Insurance	.	Penn General Insurance	Scotland
Pioneer Life	.	Penn Genl SVEC of Michigan	England
Presidential Life	.		
Primerica	.	Polk & Sullivan (Nashville, TN)	England
Principal Mutual Life	.	Potomac Insurance of Illinois	Scotland
Provident Life &	.	Protective Insurance	Puerto Rico
Accident	.	(Omaha, NE)	
Prudential Insurance	.	Preferred Life of New York	Germany

Reliance Group	. Real America Investors (Iowa)	Netherlands
	. Republic Services	Swiss
	. Republic Insurance Co/	Swiss
	. Republic Vanguard Insurance	
	. (Dallas, TX)	
	. Royal Insurance	England
	. (IL/MO/NC/NY/OK)	
Safeco	. SafeGuard Insurance (NC)	England
Spartan Insurance	. Security Assurance	Puerto Rico
	. (Omaha, NE)	
State Farm	. Security Life of Denver	Netherlands
St. Paul Cos	. Sentinel Life	Canada
SunAmerica Corp	. Sequoia Insurance	Australia
	. (Menlo Park, CA)	
	. Silvey Corp (Columbus, OH)	England
	. South Central Underwriting	Netherlands
	. (Tennessee)	
	. Southland Insurance of GA	Netherlands
	. Southland Life Insurance (TX)	Netherlands
	. Southern Insurance	Swiss
	. (Dallas, TX)	
	. Southwest Equity Life (AZ)	Netherlands
	. SunLife US	Canada
	. Superior Insurance (Georgia)	Netherlands
	. Talbot Bird & Co (New York)	England
Teacher's Insurance	.	
Teledyne Insurance	.	
Tourchmark	. Tower Insurance (Wisconsin)	England
TransAmerica Corp	. Transunion Casualty (IA)	Netherlands
Travelers Insurance	.	
Corp	. Tri-State Insurance (Tulsa,OK)	England
United American	. United Finance Services (MD)	Netherlands
Unitrin	. Universal Underwriters	Swiss
	. (Shawnee, KS)	
USF&G	.	
US Life Corp	. Vanguard Insurance	Swiss
	. (Dallas, TX)	
Western & Southern	. Western America Insurance	England
Life	.	
Western Life	. Western Life Insurance (MN)	Netherlands
Assurance	.	

A. L. Williams Ins	. Western Time Insurance (WI)	Netherlands
	. Western Union Security Life	Netherlands
	. (Georgia)	
	. Western States Insurance (ND)	Canada
	. Wisconsin National Life	England
	. Wisconsin National Life Ins	Netherlands
	. William Penn	England
Xerox Financial	. Willis Corroon	England
Services Life Ins	.	

Loopholes in federal laws allow U.S. government officials to be royally entertained by foreign lobbyists but not by American lobbyists. Once the official leaves government service, there are no rules.

The U.S. Justice Department attorney in charge of extraditing Colombian cocaine dealers to the United States during the early 80s quit and now works for Colombia's Cali cocaine cartel.

The Assistant Secretary of Defense for International Affairs from 1981-1987 influenced the U.S.' $600 million military aid program to Turkey. After leaving office, he worked for Turkey securing U.S. military and economic aid.

In 1986, the Deputy Assistant Secretary of the Commerce Department led the U.S. negotiating team for sensitive trade negotiations with four Asian countries. He knew the U.S. position and game plan. Days before the scheduled talks, he quit and went to work for a Washington lobbying firm representing those four countries. He attended the meeting as an adviser to Hong Kong.

Ten former top IRS officials, including two former commissioners and a Director of the Treasury, Office of International Tax Affairs, now represent a virtual Who's Who of foreign industry against claims by the U.S. government that these foreign-owned companies underpaid their U.S. taxes by billions of dollars.

In *Agents of Influence*, Pat Choate lists the names of 200 high-ranking officials who left our government and went to work as lobbyists for foreign governments or foreign companies. The list includes six senators, nine representatives, eight special assistants to the president, five assistants to the president and four retired generals.

CHAPTER 6

HEALTH AND BEAUTY

COSMETICS AND PERFUMES

AMERICAN OWNED	FOREIGN OWNED	
Almay		
Anne Klein		
Avon	Aziza	Unilever*
Charlie	Charles of the Ritz	France
Clarion	Chloe	Unilever*
Clinique		
Coty		
Cover Girl	Dior	France
Estee Lauder	Elizabeth Arden	Unilever*
	Elizabeth Taylor/Passion	Unilever*
	Erno Laszlo	England
	Eternity	Unilever*
	Faberge	Unilever*
	Fendi	France
	Germaine Monteil	Germany
Giorgio	Givenchy	France
	Helena Rubenstein	France
	Lagerfeld	Unilever*
	Lancome	France
	L'Oreal	France
Mary Kay		
Max Factor		
Maybelline		
Natural Wonder		
Noxzema	Obsession	Unilever*
	Oscar de la Renta	France
	Perry Ellis	France
	Physicians Formula Cos.	France
	Pond's	Unilever*

* Unilever is a joint venture of England and Netherlands

Princess Marcello	. Prince Matchabelli	Unilever*
Borghese	.	
Revlon	. Shiseido	Japan
Ultima II	. Visible Difference	Unilever*
	. Yves St. Laurent	France

CREAMS AND SKIN CARE

AMERICAN OWNED	FOREIGN OWNED	
Almay	. Albolene	England
Avon	. Andrew Jergens	Japan
Clinique	. Calgon	England
Deep Magic Lotion	.	
Estee Lauder	. Elizabeth Arden	Unilever*
	. Erno Laszlo	Unilever*
Germaine Monteil	.	
Jean Nate	.	
Lubriderm Lotion	. Lancome	France
Noxzema	. Neet	England
Oil of Olay	.	
Phisoderm	. Pond's	Unilever*
Princess Marcella	.	
Borghese	.	
Revlon	.	
SeaBreeze	.	
Soft Sense	.	
Suave	.	
Ultima II	. Vaseline	Unilever*

* Unilever is a joint venture of England and Netherlands

DEODORANTS

AMERICAN OWNED	FOREIGN OWNED	
Almay	.	
Arrid	. Babe	Unilever*
Ban	. Brut	Unilever*
Degree	.	
Dry Idea	.	
Jean Nate	.	
Ladies Choice	.	
Mitchum	.	
Mum	.	
Old Spice	.	
Right Guard	.	
Secret	.	
Soft & Dry	.	
Speed Stick	.	
Suave	.	
Sure	.	

RAZORS

AMERICAN OWNED	FOREIGN OWNED	
American Safety Razor	.	
Atra	.	
Braun	. Bic	France
Daisy	.	
Flicker	.	
GEM	.	
Gillette	.	
Good News	. Lady Schick (electric)	Netherlands
LegMate	. Norelco	Netherlands
Personal Touch	.	
Personna II	. Profile	Sweden
Remington	.	
Schick	.	
Sensor	. Smooth Operator	Japan
Trac II	. Ultraglide	Sweden
Ultrex Plus	. Wilkinson Sword	Sweden

SHAVING CREAM AND AFTERSHAVE

AMERICAN OWNED		FOREIGN OWNED	
Aramis	.	Aqua Velva	England
Barbasol	.	Brut	Unilever*
Colgate	.	Calvin Klein	Unilever*
	.	Chaps	France
Edge	.		
Gillette	.		
Halston	.		
Mennen	.		
Noxema	.		
Old Spice	.	Polo	France
	.	Ralph Lauren	France
Savoy	.	Santa Fe	Japan
Shulton of Great Britain	.		
Stetson/Coty	.	Williams Lectric Shave	England

SHAMPOO

AMERICAN OWNED		FOREIGN OWNED	
Adorn	.		
Agree	.		
Almay	.		
Avon	.		
Breck	.		
Clairol	.		
Finesse	.	Elizabeth Arden	Unilever*
Flex	.	Faberge Organics	Unilever*
Formula 405	.		
Freeman	.		
Fuller Brush	.		
Ginza	.		

* Unilever is a joint venture of England and Netherlands

AMERICAN OWNED	FOREIGN OWNED	
Head & Shoulders		
Helene Curtis		
Jean Nate		
Jhirmack		
Johnson's Baby Shampoo	Lancome	France
Neutragena	L'Oreal	France
Nexxus		
Pert		
Prell	Rave	Unilever*
Red Ken		
Revlon		
Salon Selectives		
Selsun		
Silkience		
Suave		
Ultima II		
Vidal Sassoon		
White Rain	Wella Balsam	Germany

HAIR CARE

AMERICAN OWNED	FOREIGN OWNED	
Adorn		
Alberto Culver	AquaNet	Unilever*
Breck		
Clairol		
Conair		
Final Net		
Finesse		
Flex		
Free Style		
Helene Curtis	L'Oreal	France
Salon Selectives	Preference	France
Suave		
White Rain		

* Unilever is a joint venture of England and Netherlands

MEN'S HAIR CARE

AMERICAN OWNED	FOREIGN OWNED	
	. Brylcreem	England
Dry Look	. Groom & Clean	Unilever*
Protein 29	. Score	England
Top Brass	. Vaseline Hair Tonnic	Unilever*
VO5	. Vitalis	England

SOAPS AND BATH PRODUCTS

AMERICAN OWNED	FOREIGN OWNED	
Camay	. Calgon	England
Cashmere Bouquet	. Caress	Unilever
Coast	. Clarins Skin Care	France
Dial	. Dove	Unilever*
Irish Spring	.	
Ivory	. Lever 2000	Unilever*
Lava	. Lifebuoy	Unilever*
	. Lux	Unilever*
Pure & Natural	.	
Safeguard	. Shield	Unilever*
Tone	. Vitabath	England
Woodbury	.	
Zest	.	

TOOTHPASTE AND MOUTHWASH

Act	. Aim	Unilever*
	. Aqua-Fresh	England
	. Binanca	Swiss
Cepacol	.	
Colgate	. Close-Up	Unilever*
Crest	.	

* Unilever is a joint venture of England and Netherlands

Efferdent	.	
Gleem	.	
Interplak	.	
Lavoris	.	
Listerine	. Macleans	England
Oral B	.	
Pearl Drops	. Pepsodent	Unilever*
Reach Toothbrush	.	
Scope	. Signal	Unilever*
Ultrabrite	.	
Viadent/Vipont	.	

VITAMINS

AMERICAN OWNED	FOREIGN OWNED	
Centrum	. Bugs Bunny Vitamins	Germany
Golden Sun	. Flintstones	Germany
Lifeline	. Meritene	Swiss
	. Nature Made (Los Angeles)	Japan
	. One-A-Day	Germany
Springfield	. Shaklee	Japan
Theragram	. Sunkist Children's	
	. Chewables	Swiss

NAIL CARE

AMERICAN OWNED	FOREIGN OWNED	
	. Aziza	Unilever*
Cover Girl	. Cutex	Unilever*
Max Factor	. L'Oreal	France
Revlon	.	
Sally Hansen	.	

* Unilever is a joint venture of England and Netherlands

OVER-THE-COUNTER MEDICINES

AMERICAN OWNED	FOREIGN OWNED	
Advil	.	
Afrin	.	
Anacin	. Alka-Seltzer	Germany
Band-Aid	. Bactine	Germany
Bayer	.	
Ben-Gay	.	
Bromo Seltzer	.	
Bufferin	. Contac	England
Comtrex	. Cutter	Germany
Dristan	.	
Excedrin	. Empirin	England
	. Geritol	England
Hall's Lozenges	. Hold Cough Drops	England
Imodium A-D	.	
Medipren	. Maalox	France
	. (marketed by P&G/American)	
Metamucil	. Mentholatum	Japan
Motrin	. Mylanta	Germany
	. (with J&J/American)	
Nuprin	. Neosporin	England
Nyquil	. N'ice	England
Panadol	. Q-Tips	Unilever*
Pepto-Bismol	.	
Phillips' Milk of Mag.	.	
Prep H	.	
Premarin	.	
Robitussin	.	
Rolaids	.	
Sinaid	. Sominex	England
St. Joseph's Children's.	Sucrets	England
	. Sudafed	England
Tampax	. Tagamet	England
Tylenol	. Triaminic	Swiss
	. Tums	England
Vanquish	. Valium	Swiss
Vicks	. Vaseline	Unilever*
Visine	. Zantac	England

PHARMACEUTICAL COMPANIES

AMERICAN OWNED	FOREIGN OWNED	
Abbott Labs	. A. L. Labs	Norway
American Home Prods..		
(A.H. Robins/	.	
Wyeth Labs)	.	
Barnes & Hind	. Bayer AG	Germany
Baxter Intl. Inc	.	
Bradley Western Ind.	.	
Bristol Meyers Squibb	. Ciba Geigy	Swiss
Eli Lilly	.	
Forest Labs	. Fisons PLC	England
	. Gen Probe	Japan
	. Glaxo Holdings	England
Hewlett Packard	. Helm Pharmaceuticals	Germany
	. Hoechst-Toussel AG	Germany
ICN	. Hoffmann LaRoche	Swiss
	. (Genentech)	
Johnson & Johnson	. Lark Labs	Italy
(Ortho Labs)	.	
Marion Merrell Dow	.	
McKesson	. Miles Labs	Germany
Mead Johnson	.	
Merck	.	
Monsanto (G.D.Searle)	.	
Mylan Labs	.	
Norwich Eaton	. Norcliff Thayer	England
Pfizer Inc.	. Rhone-Poulene	France
Richardson Vicks	. Rimmel Inc.	Unilever*
	. Rorer	France
	. Sandoz	Swiss
Schering-Plough	. Schering AG	Germany
	. Schieffelind	France
	. Schmid Lab	England
	. Shaklee	Japan
	. Sigma Tau	Italy
Sterling Drugs	. Smith Klein Beecham	England

Stiefiel Labs   .
Upjohn   .
Warner Lambert   . Webber Inc.   Canada
Whithall Labs   .
Wyeth-Ayers Labs   .

Fuzzy Logic is another exciting new technology that originated in America and is being profitably produced by our foreign competitors. Fuzzy Logic is software that allows machines and computors to "think" like humans in imprecise terms, such as almost, sort of, about, nearly.

Developed by Lotfa Zadeh, a professor at UC Berkeley, the concept was either ignored or ridiculed by U.S. scientists and industry. Our foreign competitors welcomed the idea. There are more than 2,000 Fuzzy Logic patents in the hands of foreign manufacturers, and an ever-growing list of products flooding foreign markets.

There is a washing machine with more than 600 cycle combinations yet only one button - start. The machine uses an optical sensor to determine water temperature, speed and length of the cycle, and the amount of detergent needed.

A Fuzzy Logic vacuum cleaner gauges the condition of the floor and adjusts suction, and Fuzzy Logic air conditioners adapt to the number of people in the room.

Fuzzy Logic VCRs are programmed by voice commands and Fuzzy Logic TVs adjust color, brightness, sharpness and contrast every sixtieth of a second. Foreign autos have Fuzzy Logic in their automatic transmissions and suspension systems, and there is a Fuzzy Logic car capable of parking itself.

Chapter 7

HOME AND OFFICE

CLEANING PRODUCTS

AMERICAN OWNED	FOREIGN OWNED	
Ajax	. Airwick	England
Borateem	.	
Brillo Pads	.	
Comet	. Choreboy	Swiss
Dow Cleaner	.	
Drano	.	
Endust	. Easy-Off	England
Fantastik	.	
Formula 409	.	
(28% Germany)	.	
Fuller Brush	.	
GlassMates	.	
Glass Plus	.	
Grease Relief	.	
Janitor in a Drum	.	
Johnson Wax	.	
Liquid Plumber	.	
(28% Germany)	.	
Lysol	.	
Mr. Clean	.	
Parsons Ammonia	.	
Pinesol	.	
(28% Germany)	.	
Scotchbrite	. Scrub Free	Germany
Scott's Liquid Gold	. SOS Pads	Germany
SnoBol Cleaner	.	
Soft Scrub	.	
(28% Germany)	.	
Spic and Span	.	
Top Job	. Spray 'n Vac	England
Windex	.	
WD-40	.	

LAUNDRY

AMERICAN OWNED	FOREIGN OWNED	
Ajax	. ALL	Unilever*
Arm & Hammer	.	
BIZ Bleach	.	
Bold	.	
Bounce	.	
Cheer	. Cling Free Fabric Softner	Germany
Clorox (28% Germany)	.	
Cold Power	.	
Dash	. Delicare	Germany
Downy	.	
Dreft	.	
Dynamo 2	.	
ERA	.	
Fab	. Final Touch	Unilever*
Fresh Start	.	
Ivory Snow	.	
Magic Starch	.	
Niagara Spray Starch	. National Starch	Unilever*
Oxydol	.	
Punch	.	
Purex	. Rinso	Unilever*
Spray 'n Wash	. Snuggle	Unilever*
Tide	. Surf	Unilever*
	. Wisk	Unilever*
	. Woolite	England

DISHWASHING DETERGENTS

AMERICAN OWNED	FOREIGN OWNED	
Ajax	. ALL	Unilever*
Cascade	.	
Crystal White Octagon	.	
Dawn	. Dove	Unilever*

Dermassage	.	Electrasol	Germany
Ivory Liquid	.		
Joy	.	Jet Dry	Germany
Palmolive	.		
Pathmark	.		
Sweetheart	.	Sunlight	Unilever*
White Magic	.		

* Unilever is a joint venture of England and Netherlands

MAJOR APPLIANCES

The United States government pays $24 billion just in interest payments to foreigners, more than it spends on education.

REFRIGERATORS

AMERICAN OWNED		FOREIGN OWNED	
Admiral	.		
Amana	.		
Caloric	.		
Coldspot	.	Frigidaire	Sweden
General Electric	.	Gibson	Sweden
Hot Point	.		
Jenn-Air	.		
Kenmore	.		
KitchenAid	.	Kelvinator	Sweden
Magic Chef	.		
Roper	.	Philco	Sweden
Sub-Zero	.	Tappan	Sweden
Whirlpool	.	White Westinghouse	Sweden

RANGE/OVENS

AMERICAN OWNED		FOREIGN OWNED
Admiral	.	
Amana	.	
Caloric	.	
Corning	.	

AMERICAN OWNED	FOREIGN OWNED	
General Electric	. Frigidaire	Sweden
Hardwick	. Gibson	Sweden
Hot Point	.	
Kenmore	. Kelvinator	Sweden
KitchenAid	.	
Magic Chef	.	
Maytag	. Nutone	England
Radar Range	.	
Roper	.	
Thermador	. Tappan	Sweden
Whirlpool	. White Westinghouse	Sweden

MICROWAVE

AMERICAN OWNED	FOREIGN OWNED	
Amana	. Brother	Japan
GE	. Goldstar	Korea
Hot Point	.	
Kenmore	.	
KitchenAid	.	
Litton	.	
Magic Chef	. Matsushita	Japan
JC Penney	. Panasonic	Japan
Roper	. Quasar	Japan
	. Samsung	Korea
	. Sanyo	Japan
	. Sharp	Japan
	. Tappan	Sweden
	. Toshiba	Japan
Whirlpool	. White Westinghouse	Sweden

VACUUM CLEANERS

AMERICAN OWNED	FOREIGN OWNED	
Bissell	.	
	. Electrolux	Sweden
Filter Queen	. Eureka	Sweden
Hoover	. Fisker	Denmark
Kirby	.	

Kwik Sweep	.		
Oreck	.	Panasonic	Japan
Royal	.	Regina	Sweden
Sears Kenmore	.	Rexair	England
(made in Japan)	.		
Sunbeam	.	Sharp	Japan
	.	White Westinghouse	Sweden

SEWING MACHINES

AMERICAN OWNED		FOREIGN OWNED	
	.	Bernina	Swiss
	.	Brother	Japan
	.	Elna	Sweden
	.	Necchi	Italy
	.	Nelco	Japan
	.	Pfaff	Germany
	.	Riccar	Japan
Sears Kenmore	.	Singer (made in Taiwan)	Hong Kong
(made in Japan and	.		
Taiwan)	.		
Simplicity	.	Viking	Sweden
	.	White	Sweden

AIR CONDITIONERS

AMERICAN OWNED		FOREIGN OWNED	
AirTemp	.		
Amana	.		
Borg Warner	.		
Carrier	.		
Climatrol	.		
Counselor	.	Daiken	Japan
Fedders	.	Emerson	Sweden
Friedrich	.	Gibson	Sweden
GE	.		
HotPoint	.		
Kenmore	.		
Lennox	.	Mitsubishi	Japan

			Japan
	.	Panasonic	Japan
	.	Sanyo	Japan
	.	Sharp	Japan
Whirlpool	.	White Westinghouse	Sweden

HOUSEWARES AND SMALL APPLIANCES

AMERICAN OWNED		FOREIGN OWNED	
Anchor Hocking	.	AMS (plastic housewares)	England
Black & Decker	.	Ansell	Australia
Braun	.		
Club Cooker	.		
Conair	.		
Corningware	.		
Ekco	.		
Emhart	.	Farberware	England
Graniteware	.		
Hefty Designs	.	Hamilton Beach	Ireland
Hobart	.	Hitachi	Japan
Magnalite	.		
Mirro Corp	.		
Mr. Coffee	.		
Mixmaster	.		
NordicWare	.	Norelco	Netherlands
	.	Nutone	England
Premark	.		
Presto	.	Panasonic	Japan
Proctor Silex/Wearever	.	.	
Pyrex	.		
Regalware	.	Regent-Shiffield	Japan
Revere Ware	.		
Rival	.		
Rubbermaid	.		
Sunbeam-Oster	.		
Toastmaster	.	Thermos	Japan
Tupperware	.		
Waring	.		
Wearever/Proctor Silex	.		
West Bend	.		

PAPER PRODUCTS: KITCHEN

AMERICAN OWNED	FOREIGN OWNED	
Big 'n Thirsty	.	
Bounty	.	
Coronet	. Comet Paper Products	Germany
Designer Sparkle	.	
Dow	.	
First Brands	.	
Hi-Dri	.	
Job Squad	.	
Reynolds	.	
Scott (24% Canada)	.	
Spillmate	.	
Viva	.	
Zee	.	

PAPER PRODUCTS: BATHROOM

AMERICAN OWNED	FOREIGN OWNED
Angel Soft	.
Charmin	.
Cottonelle	.
Family Scott	.
(24% Canada)	.
Marina	.
MD	.
Nice & Soft	.
Northern	.

SEWING NOTIONS

AMERICAN OWNED	FOREIGN OWNED
Butterick Patterns	.
McCall's Patterns	.
Simplicity Patterns	.

Vogue Patterns	.		
American Thread	.	Coats & Clarke Thread	England
	.	DMC Thread	France
	.	Scoville Zippers	Canada
	.	Talon Zippers	England
Wright (notions)	.	Thompson of California (fabrics)	Japan
	.	ZKK Zippers	Japan

KNIVES AND SCISSORS

AMERICAN OWNED		FOREIGN OWNED	
Ekco	.	Fiskars	Finland
Revere	.	Regent Sheffield	Japan
Walnut Knives	.	Wilkinson Sword	Sweden

PENS AND PENCILS

AMERICAN OWNED		FOREIGN OWNED	
A. T. Cross	.		
Berol Mirado (pencils)	.	Bic Pens	France
Crayola	.		
Empire (pencils)	.		
Faber (pencils)	.		
Fendi	.		
Mark Cross	.		
Papermate (pens)	.	Parker Pens	England
	.	Pentel (pens)	France
	.	Pitol (pens)	Japan
Waterman Pens	.	Sheaffer Eaton (pens)	Swiss

TEMPORARY SERVICES

AMERICAN OWNED		FOREIGN OWNED	
Firstaff	.	First Temporaries Inc. (Maine)	England
Kelly Services	.	Jobs Temporary Inc.	England

Norell			
	.	Manpower	England
	.	OTI Services Inc. (New York)	France
Uniforce Temporary	.	Temporaries Inc. (Wash. DC)	England
Personnel	.		
Western Temp (350)	.	Talent Tree Temporaries (Texas)	England

TOOLS, HAND AND POWER

AMERICAN OWNED	FOREIGN OWNED	
Black and Decker	. Ames Lawn and Garden Tools	England
(Emhart)	.	
Channel Lock USA	.	
Cooper Tools	.	
Craftsman	.	
Crescent	.	
Danaher	.	
Easco Hand Tools	.	
Estwin USA	. Fuller Tools	Japan
Lawn-Boy	.	
Lufkin	.	
Newell Tools	.	
Nickolson	.	
Olympia Industries	.	
(made in Taiwan)	.	
Plumb	. Roper	Sweden
Skil	. SKF Tools	Sweden
Snapper Power Equip.	.	
Stanley Tools	.	
Toro	. Traub Tools	Germany
True Temper Lawn	.	
and Garden	.	
Vaughn USA	.	
Vermont American	.	
Corp	.	
Weller	. Weed Eater	Sweden
Wiss	.	

SEEDS

AMERICAN OWNED	FOREIGN OWNED	
W. Atlee Burpee	. Armstrong Roses	Japan
	. Ciba Geigy Seeds	Swiss
	. Fredonia Seed Company	Canada
	. Germaine Inc Seeds	England
	. International Seeds (Oregon)	Netherlands
	. Jackson Perkins	Japan
	. Northrup King	Swiss
	. Stakes Seed Company	Canada
	. (Niagara Falls, NY)	

GARDEN SUPPLIES

AMERICAN OWNED	FOREIGN OWNED	
Gaviota	. Jiffy Products	Swiss
Miracle Gro	. Northrup King	Swiss
Orkin Lawn Care	. Sencor Weed Killer	Germany
Ortho Products	. Spectrum Lawn Care	Swiss
Roundup	.	

INSECT SPRAY

AMERICAN OWNED	FOREIGN OWNED	
	. Black Flag	England
Combat	.	
(28% Germany)	.	
	. Holiday Insecticide	England
Raid	. Spectrum	Unilever*

* Unilever is a joint venture of England and Netherlands

Foreign-owned companies receive U.S. government benefits and incentives rarely offered to American-owned companies. Pennsylvania gave Germany's Volkswagen a total package worth $86 million to open an assembly plant in New Stanton, Pennsylvania. The package included a $40 million loan at 1.75% interest for the first 20 years, increasing to 4%, $30 million for a road link and railway spur, a $3.8 million training program, a five-year county property-tax abatement and a state designation of the plant site as a foreign-trade sub-zone. That cost the people of Pennsylvania about $8,000 for each new job. Less than ten years later, Volkswagen closed the plant, and Pennsylvania waived the $40 million owed.

Two years later, it started all over. Pennsylvania gave Sony Corporation a package of approximately $25.5 million in grants and and low-interest loans to open a television picture tube factory in that same plant.

No incentives were ever offered to Zenith, the only American-owned television manufacturer.

Chapter 8

STORES

RETAIL DEPARTMENT STORES

AMERICAN OWNED	FOREIGN OWNED	
Alexander's (11)	. Abraham & Straus (14)	Canada
Ames	. Allied Stores	Canada
Amfac/Liberty House	.	
Associated Dry Goods	.	
Bergdorf Goodman(17)	.	
Bon-Ton Stores (33)	.	
Broadway (43)	. Bloomingdales (17)	Canada
(So. California)	.	
Broadway Southwest	. The Bon/Bon Marche (39)	Canada
(11)	.	
	. Bonwit Teller (16)	Australia
	. Brooks Brothers	England
	. Bullocks	Canada
	. Burdine's (30)	Canada
Dayton Hudson (37)	.	
Dillard Dept. (162)	. Donaldson's	Swiss
Emporium Capwell's	.	
(22)	.	
Famous-Barr	. Frederick and Nelson	England
Feline's Boston	.	
Foley's (Texas)	.	
G. Fox	.	
G&G	. Garfinkel's	Saudi Arabia
Goldwaters	. Gimbels	England
Gottschalks	. Goldsmith's	Canada
Hecht's	. Harris Co. (California)	Spain
I. Magnin (30)	.	
Ivey's (23)	.	
Jacobson Stores (22)	. Jordan Marsh (26)	Canada
Joslins	. Joske's	Netherlands
Kaufmann's	. Korvettes	France
Liberty House	. Laura Ashley	England

	Foreign owned	Country
Lord & Taylor (51)	Lazarus (43)	Canada
	Lodge Apparel	Netherlands
Macy's	Maaz Brothers (38)	Canada
Marshalls Inc.	Maurice Apparel	Netherlands
Marshall Fields (24)	Miller and Rhods	England
May Company (324)	Millers	England
Meier & Frank		
Melvilles		
Mervyns (227)		
Montgomery Ward		
Neiman-Marcus (22)		
Nordstrom's (54)		
	James A. Ogilvy	Canada
	Ohrbach's	Netherlands
JC Penny (1355)		
Powers		
J.W. Robinson	Rich's (24)	Canada
Sears (897)	Sak's Fifth Avenue (45)	Saudi Arabia
Stewart Dry Goods	Sakowitz	Australia
	Sanger Harris	Canada
	Sharp's (Texas)	Germany
	Stern's (24)	Canada
Thalhimers (25)	Thimbles	England
Value City (53)		
Weinstock's (12)		

SPECIALTY STORES: APPAREL

AMERICAN OWNED	FOREIGN OWNED	
Abercrombie & Fitch		
Ann Taylor (185)	Anne Klein & Co.	Japan
Attivo		
Banana Republic (111)	Benetton	Italy
Carter Hawley Hale	Brooks Brothers	England
Casual Corner		
Charming Shoppes	Carson Pirie Scott (33)	Swiss
Chess King (564)	Catherine's Stout Shoppe	Canada
Cignal		
ClothesLine (349)		

Contempo Casuals (211)		
Country Miss	.	
County Seat	.	
Dejaiz	.	
T. Edwards (54)	.	
Express	. Foxmoor (600)	Canada
Gap (747)	. Gucci	Italy/Saudi Arabia
Gleneagles	. Honeybee	Germany
Hartmarx	.	
Henri Bendel	.	
Hit or Miss (534)	.	
Lane Bryant (720)	.	
Lerner Stores	.	
Limited Inc (3168)	. Loehmann's Inc.	Spain
Marianne	.	
McAlpin's	.	
Merry-Go-Round	. Michael Cromer	Germany
Mode O'Day	.	
Payless Shoe Stores	.	
(2967)	.	
Petrie Stores (1645)	.	
Rave	.	
Ross Stores (156)	.	
Silverman's	. Talbots	Japan
Victoria's Secret	. Thimbles	England
	. Town & Country Clothing	Canada
Winkelman's	. Ups 'n Downs Shoe	Canada
Wilson's (489)	. Wilkes Bashford	Japan

CONVENIENCE

<u>AMERICAN OWNED</u>   <u>FOREIGN OWNED</u>

AM/PM Mini Markets	.	
Circle K (partial)	. Circle K	Canada
	. (350 stores in WA, OR, ID, UT, MT & CO)	
Li'l Peach (63)	.	
MiniMart (960)	.	
National Convenience	.	
(1100) (Stop 'n Go)	.	
Village Pantry (168)	. 7-Eleven (6700)	Japan

BOOKSTORES

AMERICAN OWNED	FOREIGN OWNED	
,	B. Dalton (800)	Netherlands
.	Barnes & Noble	Netherlands
.	Bookstop (24)	Netherlands
Crown Books (257) .	Doubleday BookShops (39)	Netherlands
Tower Books .	Scribner's	Netherlands
Walden Books (1255) .		

SPECIALTY STORES: HARDWARE

AMERICAN OWNED	FOREIGN OWNED	
Ace Hardware .		
Builders Square .		
Builders Emporium .	Builderama Inc	England
Coast to Coast .	Central Hardware (Missouri)	Belgium
Grossman's .		
Hechinger .	Handy Andy Home	Belgium
.	Improvement Centers	
HomeClub (73) .		
Home Depot (118) .		
Lowe's (300) .		
Orchid Supply Hdwe .	Mr. Goodbuys	Netherlands
Pergament (35) .		
True Value (8500) .	Scotty's (165)	Belgium

SPECIALTY STORES: TOYS AND SPORTS

AMERICAN OWNED	FOREIGN OWNED	
ChildWorld (163) .		
Circus World .	FAO Schwartz	Netherlands
.	Herman's Sporting Goods	England
.	Intelligent Toy Store (Georgia)	England

Kay-Bee Toys and Hobby (727)	.		
Lionel (92)	.		
	.	Oshman's Sporting Goods	England
Toys R Us	.		

SPECIALTY STORES DISCOUNT

AMERICAN OWNED		FOREIGN OWNED	
Ames (371)	.		
Ben Franklin Stores	.		
Best Products	.		
Big Bear (68)	.		
BJ Wholesale Club(29)	.		
Caldor Discount (123)	.		
Consolidated Stores	.	Consumers Distributors (89)	Canada
(ODD Lots/Big Lots)	.		
Costco (69)	.		
Dollar General (1339)	.		
Family Dollar Stores	.		
(1580)	.		
Filene's Basement	.		
GEM	.		
H.L. Green	.		
Heck's (550)	.		
Hills (154)	.		
Jamesway (134)	.		
Job Lot Trading	.		
Kmart (2200)	.		
Kress	.		
McCrory	.		
McLellan	.		
Marshalls (400)	.		
Meyer's (112)	.		
G. C. Murphy	.		
JJ Newberry's	.		
Pace Membership	.		
Warehouse	.		
Phar-Mor	.		

Pic N Save (190) .	Pic & Pay Stores	Canada
Price Club .		
Ross Stores (197) .		
Rose's (259) .		
Sam's Wholesale Club .		
ShopKo (87) .		
Syms Corp (25) .		
T G & Y (625) .		
TJ Maxx (337) .		
Target (407) .		
Value City (53) .		
Venture Discount (75) .		
Waban Inc .		
Wal-Mart .	Warehouse Club	Germany
Wholesale Club Inc(28).		
Wholesale Depot .		
Woolworth/Woolco .		
(8120) .		
Zayre .		

SPECIALTY STORES: DRUGSTORES

AMERICAN OWNED	FOREIGN OWNED	
Acme Drugs .		
Arbor Drugs (87) .		
Big B Drugs .	Bud's Deep Discount Drugs	England
Civic Drug Stores .	Carl's Drugs (New York)	Australia
CVS Drugs .		
Drug Emporium (Ohio) .		
Fay's Inc (240) .		
Genovese Drug Stores .	ICI Pharmacy	England
(95) .		
Lane Drugs .		
Long's Drugstores .		
(257) .		
Osco Drugs .		
Pay 'N Save .		
Payless Drugs .		
Peoples Drug Stores .		

Perry Drug Stores (208) .
Reed Drugs (1100)   .
Revco (1100)   .
RiteAid (2429)   .
Savon Drugs   .
SCG Drugs   . Shoppers Drug Mart   Canada
Sentry Drug Stores   .
Skaggs Drugs   .
Thrift Drug Co (434) .
Walgreen (1646)   .
Welby Super Drugs   .

SPECIALTY STORES: JEWELRY

AMERICAN OWNED   FOREIGN OWNED

                   . Black, Starr & Frost   England
                   . Gordon's   Canada
                   . J.B. Robinson   England
                   . Kay Jewelers   England
                   . Marcus & Co   England
                   . Merksamer Jewelers   Australia
                   . Ratners (473)   England
                   . Sterling   England
                   . Tiffany's/Hawaii   Japan
                   . Tiffany's (10)   (14%) Japan
                   . Weisfield Inc   England
                   . Zale's   Canada/Swiss

SPECIALTY STORES: OTHER

AMERICAN OWNED	FOREIGN OWNED	
Fox Photo	. Fotomat	Japan
	. RentaCenter	England
	. Video Station	Netherlands

America is the only industrialized country that allows foreign investment without any process of review or approval. Unless national security is involved, foreign investors do not even register their activities. Sixteen federal agencies track different aspects of foreign investment, but they do not coordinate their data, and some keep their information secret - even from Congress.

Great Britain reviews all takeovers in "important" manufacturing concerns, and the French government must approve all investments with more than 20% foreign ownership of a French firm.

In South Korea, foreign investors are limited to 15% ownership and strictly prohibited from more than a third of the country's industries.

Australia will reject a foreign investor if there is an Australian ready to invest "at reasonable terms and conditions."

Mexico forbids foreign ownership of border or costal land, and other land can be held in trust but must ultimately be sold to a Mexican National.

In Canada, foreign-owned banks are limited to one main office and one branch, and the total assets of all foreign banks cannot exceed 8% of the total domestic assets of Canadian-owned banks.

Japan has the strictest investment approval process, and in many industries only joint ventures, with a Japanese national, are permitted.

Chapter 9

REAL ESTATE

Foreign money does not enlarge the tax base. A House subcommittee investigation of 36 foreign-owned U.S. companies found that more than half paid little or no U.S. income tax during a 10-year period. An IRS study showed that American-owned manufacturers' taxable income was 4.3% of U.S. sales, while foreign-owned manufacturers' taxable income was 1.7% of U.S. sales.

FOREIGN OWNED LANDMARKS/REAL ESTATE

ALABAMA

Birmingham	. International Park	Finland

ARIZONA

Castle Rock	. Plum Creek	Canada
Mesa	. The Crossings	Japan
	. Park Plaza	Japan
Phoenix	. Camelback Esplanade	Japan
	. One Columbus Plaza	Canada
	. Home Federal Tower	Canada
Tempe	. Westcourt in the Buttes	Japan

CALIFORNIA

Alameda	. Parkway Center	Canada
Anaheim	. State College Plaza	Japan
Belmont	. Island Park	Japan
Beverly Hills	. I.Magnin Building	Japan
	. LaColonnade	Japan
	. Two Rodeo Drive	Japan
Burbank	. Triad Center	Japan
	. The Burbank Tower	Japan

Calabasas	. Calabasas Country Club	Japan
Century City	. 1900 & 1901 Ave. of Stars	Japan
Claremont	. College Business Park	Japan
Cupertino	. Vallco Fashion Park	Australia
Delano	. Panadol's Citrus Grove	England
El Segundo	. Hughes Aircraft Building	Japan
Freemont	. Xidex Building	Japan
Fresno	. First Interstate Bank Bldg.	Japan
Garden Grove	. Industrial Bldg.	Korea
Glendale	. 505 North Brand Boulevard	Japan
Hemet	. Seven Hills	Japan
	. Sears Savings Bank Building	Japan
Irvine	. Burlington Air Express Building	Japan
	. Crocker Bank Center	Japan
	. Irvine Commercial Center	Japan
La Jolla	. Aventine	Japan
Long Beach	. Shoreline Square	Japan
Los Angeles	. Arco Plaza	Japan
	. Asian Trade Center	Australia
	. AT&T Building	Japan
	. Atlantic Richfield Hdqrtrs	Japan
	. (contains BankAmerica So.	
	. California Headquarters)	
	. Broadway Plaza	Japan
	. California Bank Building	Japan
	. Chase Plaza	Japan
	. Citicorp West Coast Hdqrtrs.	Japan
	. Coast Federal Building	Japan
	. 901 Corporate Center	Japan
	. El Rancho Verde Country Club	Japan
	. 865 Figueroa Street	Canada
	. Guardian Bank Building	Japan
	. Manulife Plaza	Japan
	. Citicorp Phases II & III	Japan
	. Riviera Country Club	Japan
	. Texaco Building	Korea
	. The Enclave	Japan
	. 777 Tower	Japan
	. Triad Center	Japan
	. Union Bank Building	Japan
	. One Westwood Building	England
	. One Wilshire Boulevard	Canada

	. 800 Wilshire Boulevard	Japan
	. 1000 Wilshire Boulevard	Japan
	. World Trade Center	Japan
Manhattan Beach	. 225 So. Sepulveda Boulevard	Japan
Marin	. Larkspur Landing	Japan
Martinez	. One Summit Centre	Korea
Monterey	. Pebble Beach Golf Courses	Japan
Napa	. Silverado Country Club	Japan
Newbury Park	. Hillcrest Center	Germany
Newport Beach	. Westerly Place	Japan
Oakland	. Wells Fargo Building	Japan
Ontario	. Plaza Continental	Japan
Pacific Palisades	. Riviera Country Club	Japan
Palm Springs	. Mesquite Country Club	Japan
	. Mission Hills Country Club	Canada
Pasadena	. Coast Savings Bank	Japan
San Bernardino/	. Milliken Business Center	Netherlands
Orange County	. Sunnymead Ranch	France
San Diego	. Emerald-Shapery Center	Japan
	. Kona Kai Club	Australia
	. La Costa Country Club	Japan
San Francisco	. 101 California Street	Japan
	. GoldenGate Field's Race Track	England
	. Harbor Bay Community	Japan
	. 505 Montgomery Street	Japan
	. 611 Montgomery Street	Hong Kong
	. 100 Spear Street	Japan
	. 111 Sutter Street	Japan
	. 500 Washington Building	Japan
	. Robert Dollar Building	Japan
	. South Beach Marina	Canada
San Jose	. Country Club Heights	Canada
	. Creekside Townhouse	Canada
Santa Ana	. 1821 Dyer Road	Japan
	. 3 Hutton Center Drive	Japan
	. Peppertree	Canada
Santa Monica	. 100 Wilshire Boulevard	Japan
Sherman Oaks	. Mulholland Estates Devlpmnt	Hong Kong
Sonoma County	. Westwind Business Park	Italy
Vista	. Industrial Park	Japan
Walnut Creek	. 2700 Ygnacio Road	Japan

COLORADO

Aurora	. Pavilion Towers	Japan
Breckenridge	. Breckenridge Skiing Co.	Japan
Denver	. One Denver Place	Canada
	. Pavilion Tower	Japan
Steamboat Springs	. Steamboat Springs Ski Resort	Japan

CONNECTICUT

East Hartford	. Founder Plaza	Netherlands
Greenwich	. 33 Benedict Place	Anglo/Dutch
New Haven	. Government Center	Canada
Stamford	. Harbor Park	Japan

FLORIDA

Broward	. Commercial Point Shop.Center	Canada
South Dade County	. Calusa Country Club	Japan
Harbour Island	. One Harbour Place	Singapore
Miami	. The Babylon	Venezuela
	. 9551 Collins Avenue	Canada
	. Cocowalk	France
	. Courvoisier Center	Hong Kong
	. Freedom Tower	Saudia Arabia
	. Greenleaf Resort	Japan
	. Indian River Citrus Grove	Japan
	. Manhattan Tower	Canada
	. 259 SW 13th Street	Haiti
	. Winston Tower Apartments	Canada
New Port Richey	. Towne Center Shopping Plaza	Canada
North Miami Beach	. Turnberry Yacht & Cntry Club	Hong Kong
	. Waterways Condominium	Canada
Orlando	. Norwegian Pavilion	Canada
	. Olympia Place Tower	Canada
River Beach	. Marina	Canada
Tampa	. 501 Madison Street	England
	. Rocky Point Island Center	Canada

GEORGIA

Atlanta	. Atlanta Tradeport FTZ	Netherlands
	. Coastal States Building	England
	. Connally Building	Japan
	. Corporex Center	Sweden
	. Gateway office Building	Australia
	. IBM Tower	Japan
	. Market Square	Canada
	. Metropolitan Club	Japan
	. Palisades	Netherlands
	. 191 Peachtree Tower	Netherlands
	. Snap Finger Woods Club	Japan
	. South Meadow Industrial Park	England
	. TradePort	Japan
	. The Walton Apartments	Canada
	. Valdosta Mall	England
	. Westlake Industrial Park	England
Brunswick	. Glynn Place Mall	England
East Point	. Camp Creek Business Center	England
Fulton County	. Ammersee on the Chattahoochi	Germany
Duluth	. Esplanade Mall	England
Gainesville	. Lake Shore Mall	England
Morrow	. Summit at SouthLake	England
Sandy Springs	. Centrum	Netherlands
Suwanee	. Shawnez Ridge	Australia
Union City	. Union Station Apartments	Germany

ILLINOIS

Chicago	. AT&T Corporate Center	Japan
	. Avondale Center	Japan
	. Cigna Building	Sweden
	. The Esplanade	Japan

.	222 North LaSalle	Sweden
.	142 E. Ontario	Canada
.	One Prudential Plaza Bldg	Japan
.	Two Prudential Tower	Japan
.	Quaker Tower	Japan
.	One Sansome Street	Japan
.	USG Corporate Headquarters	Canada
.	101 North Wacker Drive	Japan
.	225 West Wacker Drive	Japan
.	Zerox Center	Japan

INDIANA

Indianapolis	. Forum at the Crossing	Japan

KENTUCKY

Lexington	. Chinoe Village	England

MAINE

Bangor	. Bangor Mall	Canada

MARYLAND

Baltimore	. Commerce Place	Japan
	. Harborview	Singapore
Calvert	. Bay View Hills	Australia
Forestville	. Presidential Corporate Center	England

MASSACHUSETTS

Boston	.	
	. Devonshire Building	Ireland
	. Exchange Place Building	Japan
	. 265 Franklin Street	England
	. Five Hundred Boylston	Netherlands
	. LaFayette Place	Swiss
	. One Liberty Square	England
	. 101 Merrimac Street 1	England
	. 71 Newbury Street	England
	. Paine Webber Building	Japan

	.	Scotch & Sirloin Building	England
	.	One Washington Mall	Japan
	.	One Winthrop Square	Netherlands
Springfield	.	One Financial Place	Canada
Waltham	.	Somerset Court	England

MINNESOTA

Minneapolis	.	Northstar Center	Canada

MONTANA

Dillon	.	Lazy 8 Ranch	Japan

NEW JERSEY

Bedminster	.	CityFed Building	Japan
Cavin Point	.	Port Liberty	Swiss
Edgewater	.	Yaohan Plaza	Japan
Lakewood	.	Leisure Park	Japan
Lawrenceville	.	Kings Brook Country Estate	England
	.	Quaker-Bridge Mall	Canada

NEW YORK

Buffalo	.	Fountain Plaza	Canada
New York City	.	ABC Building	Japan
	.	American Towers	Japan
	.	Battery Park City Project	Canada
	.	60 Broad Street	Hong Kong
	.	Chamber of Commerce Bldg	Taiwan
	.	Citicorp Bank Building	Japan
	.	Exxon Building	Japan
	.	461 Fifth Avenue	Japan
	.	666 Fifth Avenue	Japan
	.	Gift Mart Building	Japan
	.	Hudson River Center	Brussels
	.	ITT Building	Japan
	.	One Liberty Plaza	Canada
	.	275 Madison Avenue	Japan
	.	Mellon Financial Center	Japan
	.	Memphis Downtown	England

	. Mobil Oil Building	Japan
	. NewYork City Corp Center	Japan
	. Paine Webber Building	Japan
	. Park Avenue Plaza	Japan
	. Rockefeller Center	Japan
	. (NBC Studios/Radio City Music	
	. Hall/Time Life Building)	
	. Saatachi & Saatchi Building	Sweden
	. 900 Third Avenue	Japan
	. Tiffany Building	Japan
	. Tower 46 Building	Japan
	. Tower 49 Building	Japan
	. 55 Water Street	Canada
	. World Financial Center	Canada
	. World Wide Plaza	Japan

NORTH CAROLINA

| Hickory | . First Union Bank Building | France |

OHIO

| Cincinnati | . L.S.Ayres & Co. Buildings | Netherlands |
| Fairfield | . Forest Fair Mall | Australia |

OREGON

Clackamas County	. Sunnyside Plaza	Canada
H. Byden Island	. Hillman Properties	Japan
Portland	. 621 SW Adler Building	New Zealand
	. 512 SW Broadway Building	Japan
	. Boise Cascade Building	New Zealand
	. Exchange Building	New Zealand
	. Forest Park Eschange	Nauru
	. Frederick & Nelson Building	New Zealand
	. Lake Oswego Apt. Complex	Japan
	. Madison Tower	Swiss
	. Multnoman Apartments	Canada
	. River Place	Japan
	. The Vinyards	Japan
	. Wilcox Building	New Zealand
	. Willamette Building	Japan

PENNSYLVANIA

Allentown	. Lehigh Valley Mall	Canada
	. Whitehall Mall	Canada
Philadelphia	. One Logan Square	Canada
	. The Windsor	Japan
King of Prussia	. Court and Mall	Japan
Montgomeryville	. Montgomery Mall	Canada
	. Meadows Race Track	England
Pittsburgh	. Mellon Financial Center	Japan

TEXAS

Austin	. Lamar Financial Plaza	Japan
	. Town Lake Center	Japan
Corpus Christy	. Lake Padre Development	Germany
Dallas	. Dallas Market Center	Japan
	. Festival Marketplace	Belgium
	. One Main Plaza	Canada
	. Parkview Center	Canada
	. Southland Center	Netherlands
	. Tai Van Corp	Canada
	. Texas Commerce Bank Bldg	Canada
	. Thanksgiving Tower	Singapore
	. Willowcreek Village	Canada
Fort Worth	. Monnig's Oak Shopping Cen.	Mexico
	. Ridgemar Mall	Canada
Galveston	. Park Apartments	Australia
Houston	. Arena Tower I	
	. 397 North Belt	Belgium
	. Colonial House	Canada
	. Continental Resources Center	Japan
	. Fondrea Southwest Med. Bldg	Hong Kong
	. Four Oaks Place Center	Taiwan
	. Gulfton & Rampart Shop. Cen.	Taiwan
	. Lakeview of Cypress Station	Belgium
	. North West Crossing III	Belgium
	. One Wood Way Plaza	Belgium
	. Penzoil Place	Germany

	. Renwick Square Apartments	Australia
	. Richmond Park	Belgium
	. Southern Natl. Bank Bldg	Taiwan
	. Ten Thousand Richmond	Belgium
	. Waterford Plaza	Canada
	. Welchem Building	Belgium

UTAH

Salt Lake City	. Triad Center	Saudi Arabia

VERMONT

Stratton Mountain	. Stratton Mountain Ski Resort	Japan

VIRGINIA

Arlington	. Lincoln Place	Japan
Ballston	. Ballston Station Building	England
Roanoke	. The Summit	Finland
Rosslyn	. Plaza West	England
	. Commonwealth Building	England
Virginia Beach	. Lynwood Plaza	Germany

WASHINGTON

Bellevue	. Bellevue Place	Japan
Seattle	. AT&T Gateway Tower	Japan
	. First & Stewart Building	Japan
	. Pacific First Center	Japan

WASHINGTON D.C.

	. American Medical Assoc Bldg	Japan
	. Army Navy Club	England
	. Esplanade	Japan
	. Farragut Building	Netherlands
	. FCC Office Building	Japan
	. 555 Fourth Street	Japan
	. Judiciary Center	Japan
	. 1750 K Street NW	Japan
	. Lafayette Center	Japan

. 2025 M Street NW	Japan
. McPherson Square Building	Japan
. 1401 New York Avenue NW	Japan
. 1215 - 19th Street NW	Syria
. Olmstead Building	England
. One Thomas Circle	Japan
. Phillips Estate	Japan
. US Department of Justice	Japan
. Office Building	
. US News & World	Japan
. Report Building	
. 111 Vermont Avenue North	Japan
. Washington Square	Japan
. Watergate Complex	England

WISCONSIN

Spring Green	. Spring Green Resort	Germany

Chapter 10

HOTELS

CLOSED CIRCLE: Japanese tourists fly to Hawaii and to the U.S. mainland on Japanese airlines, take Japanese-owned tour buses to Japanese-owned hotels, eat in Japanese-owned restaurants and shop in Japanese-owned stores.

AMERICAN OWNED	FOREIGN OWNED	
Ambassador Hotel	. Algonquin Hotel	Japan
(Los Angeles)	. (New York City)	
American Motor Inns	. Allied InnKeepers	Canada
AmeriSuites	.	
Amfac Resorts		
Best Western	. Beverly Hills Hotel	Brunei
	. Beverly Wilshire	Japan
	. Biltmore Hotel (Los Angeles)	Japan
Caesars World	. Caesar Park Hotels	Japan
Clarion Htls./Rsrts.	. Chicago Hyatt Regency	Japan
	. Claridge Hotel (Chicago)	Japan
	. Clinic Inn Rochester, MN	Saudi Arabia
Colony Htls./Rsrts.	. Club Med	France
Concorde Hotels	. Concord Hilton (Oakland, CA)	Hong Kong
Continental Hotels	. Crest	England
Days Inns of Amer.	. Dana Point Resort (CA)	Japan
Desert Inn	.	
Doral Htls./Rsrts.	. Dunes Hotel & Country Club	Japan
Econo Lodges/Amer.	. Embassy Hotels	England
Embassy Suites	. Emerald Hotels	Japan
	. Embassy Suites Hotel	Japan
	. (Downey, CA/Irvine, CA)	
	. Essex House Central Park So.	Japan
	. Flordian Hotel (Tampa)	Japan
Fairmont Hotels	. Four Seasons Hotels	Canada
Golden Nugget	.	
Grand Metropltn.	. Gateway Hotels	England
Great Western	. Georgian Terrace Atlanta	Japan

	. Grand Bay Hotel Miami	Japan
	. Grand Cypress Resort (FL)	Japan
	. Grand Hotel (Houston)	England
Hampton Inn	. Hampton Inn (Key West)	Japan
Harrah's	. Hilton International	Japan
	. Holiday Civic Center	Japan
	. (San Francisco)	
	. Hollywood Roosevelt	Japan
Heritage Group	. Holiday Inn Hotels	England
Hilton Hotels	. Hospitality Inns	England
Homewood Suites	. Hotel Baronette (Michigan)	Japan
	. Hotel Bel-Air (Los Angeles)	Japan
Howard Johnson	. Hyatt Chicago	Japan
Hyatt Htls./Rsrts.	. Hyatt Grand Champions	Japan
	. Resort (Palm Springs)	
	. Hyatt Hotels in the Pacific	Japan
Imperial Hotels	. Inn on the Park	Canada
International Hotel	. (Houston, Texas)	
(Las Vegas)	. Intercontinental Hotels	Japan
	. Jefferson Hotel (Wash.DC)	Japan
Knights Inn	.	
La Quinta Motor Inn	.	
L'Ermitage Hotels	. LeMeridien Hotel Newport Bch	Hong Kong
Lexington Htl./Ste.	. Los Angeles Hilton	Korea
Loews Hotels	. J.W.Marriott Hotel	Japan
	. (CenturyCity)	
Marriott Htls./Rsrts.	. Marriott Suites (4)	Japan
	. Bethesda, MD	
	. Mark Hopkins Hotel	Japan
MGM Grand	. Mauna Kea Hotel (HI)	Japan
Mirage	. Mauna Lani Hotel (HI)	Japan
Las Vegas	. Meridien Hotels	France
	. MetHotels of Phoenix	Canada
	. Motel 6	France
	. Nassau Bay Motor Rsrt.(Hou.)	England
	. Oceanfront Hotel	Kuwait
	. (Daytona Bch)	
Outrigger Htls.Hawaii	. Omni Hotels	Hong Kong
Pacific Western Hotels	. Pan Pacific	Japan
Plaza Hotel Corp.	. Park Inns International	Japan
	. The Pierre (NY City)	Canada
Plaza Suites Hotels	. Portman Hotel (San Fran.)	Japan

Prime Motor Inns	. Prince Hotels	Japan
Promus Inc	. Princess Hotels	England
Radisson Hotel	. Ramada Inc.	Hong Kong
Red Lion Inns	.	
Red Roof Inns	.	
Regency Inns	. Regent Intl. Hotels	Japan
Resorts International	. Registry Hotel Universal City	Taiwan
Ritz Carlton	. Ritz Carlton Arlington (VA)	Japan
	. Ritz Carlton Chicago	Canada
	. Royal Concordia (New York)	Japan
	. San Franciscan Hotel	China
Select Hotels	. Sandman Hotels & Inns	Canada
	. Senator Motor Hotel (SFO)	China
Select Inns of America	. Silver Canyon (Nevada)	Japan
Sheraton Hotels, Inns	. Slumber Lodge	Canada
and Resorts	. South Coast Westin (Seattle)	Japan
Stratford House Inns	. Stanhope Hotel (New York)	Japan
Summit Hotels	. Stouffer Hotels	Swiss
Super 8 Motels	. St. Francis Hotel (Seattle)	Japan
	. St. Moritz on Park (Manhattan)	Australia
Tourway Inns of Amer.	. Town Park Hotels	England
	. TraveLodge	England
	. Travel Lounge (San Francisco)	China
	. Treadway Inns	England
	. (New Jersey, New York, Rhode Is)	
Vagabond Inns	. Vista International Hotels	England
Waldorf Astoria, NY	. Watergate Hotel (DC)	England
Wellsley Inns	. Westin Crown Plaza	Japan
	. (Kansas City, MO)	
	. Westin Hotel DC	Japan
	. Westin Renaissance (Detroit)	Japan
	. Westin San Mateo Hotel	Japan
	. Westmark Hotels	Netherlands
	. Wigwam Resort (Phoenix)	Japan
Wyndham Hotels	. Willard (Washington DC)	Japan
	. Wilsonville Holiday Inn (OR)	Japan
	. Windsor Court (New Orleans)	Bermuda

EPILOGUE

America means freedom, liberty, justice AND the power
of the individual, not as in "every man for himself," but as
"we the people" - free individuals working together.
"Ordinary people working together to achieve extraordinary
things" is a theme that runs through America's history but
never more than during World War II. All Americans were
united for a common goal. They saved, reduced consumption,
worked hard, committed to quality and deferred individual
gratification for the common good. This "can do" spirit
produced some of the greatest advances in production and
technology in history and pulled America through the war
and into a post-war standard of living that was the highest
in the world.

We must revive our "can do" spirit, our work ethic and our
spirit of teamwork, because we are again at war - an
economic war. We are witnessing the greatest transfer
of wealth outside a battlefield in the history of the world.
In the past two decades, America lost 90% of its consumer
electronics manufacturing capabilities, not by armed
combat but through economic defeats - within both the
marketplace and the American legislature. We are being
bombed with dollars and losing our lands, our industries,
and our future. We must realize that our problem is not
with foreign investors or with another country - it is with
ourselves. And the solution depends on ourselves.
Besides supporting American-owned companies, each
of us needs to make a committment to quality that will
make American products and services number one in
the world. To paraphrase Pogo:
          "We have met the solution and it is us."

While every effort has been made to verify the information herein - including contacting most of the companies listed - there may be unavoidable inaccuracies or gaps in information. This "info gap" is complicated by deliberate coverups. Furthermore, companies change ownership every day. However, this directory is as accurate as possible through October 1991.

This directory is by no means comprehensive. There is only one way to know for sure if a company or product is American-owned: ask.

I'm not anti-anybody. I'm pro-American. I'm for Economic Nationalism. It will keep America strong.

SOURCES

The following books paint a complete picture of what has happened to America and American industry and why:

Agents of Influence. Pat Choate. New York:
   Alfred A Knopf, 1990

Buying Into America. Martin and Susan Tolchin. New York:
   Berkley Books, 1989.

The End of the American Century. Steven Schlossstein.
   New York: Congdon & Weed, Inc., 1989

The Japan That Can Say No. Shintaro Ishihara. New York:
   Simon & Schuster, 1991.

*The New Competitors: How Foreign Investors Are Changing the
   U.S. Economy*.   Norman T. Glichman and Douglas P.
   Woodward. New York: Basic Books, 1989.

*Selling Out: How We Are Letting Japan Buy Our Land, Our
   Industries, Our Financial Institutions, and Our Future*.
   Douglas Frantz and Catherine Collins.
   Chicago: Contemporary Books, 1989.

Trading Places: How We Allowed Japan to Take the Lead.
   Clyde V. Prestowitz, Jr. New York: Basic Books, 1988.

Other Sources of Information:

Directory of Corporate Affiliations: Who Owns Whom,
      Wilmette, Ill.: National Registar Publishing Co., 1989.

U.S. Department of Commerce. International Trade
      Administration. *Foreign Direct Investment in the United
      States: 1986.* Washington, D.C.: U.S. Government
      Printing Office, 1987.

_____._____. *Foreign Direct Investment in the
      United States: 1987.* Washington, D.C.: U.S. Government
      Printing Office, 1988.

_____._____. *Foreign Direct Investment in the
      United States: 1988.* Washington, D.C.: U.S. Government
      Printing Office, 1989.

_____._____. *Foreign Direct Investment in the
      United States: 1989.* Washington, D.C.: U.S. Government
      Printing Office, 1991.